Bournemouth's Who Was Who

Leigh Hatts

First published in 2010 by Natula Publications
Natula Ltd., Christchurch, Dorset BH23 1JD

ISBN 9781897887813

A CIP catalogue record of this book is available from the British Library.

Printed by Cpod, Wiltshire.

The publishers would like to thank for their help and permission to reproduce their illustrations.

Bournemouth Libraries: pages 27, 28, 45, 51, 59, 72, 76, 84, 90, 113, 117, 125, 128, 131, 134, 139, 145, 158, 162, 166, 170

Bournemouth Daily Echo: page 117

The Ken Sprague Fund: page 145

Julia E Smith: page 158

All other illustrations are from the author's or publisher's collections.

Every attempt has been made by the Publisher to secure the appropriate permissions for the illustrations reproduced in this book, including where owners and copyright holders are different concerns.

If there has been any oversight we will be happy to rectify the situation. Written submission should be made to the Publisher.

Front Cover Illustration
Tower of the Royal Exeter Hotel and Poole Bay

Back Cover Illustration
The Theatre Royal, Beales and St Peter's Church from Richmond Hill

CONTENTS

	Page
LIST OF ILLUSTRATIONS	**5**
ABOUT THE AUTHOR	**7**
FOREWORD	**9**
PLACES FREQUENTLY MENTIONED	**11**
A	**15**
B	**19**
C	**36**
D	**46**
E	**55**
F	**63**
G	**68**
H	**77**
I	**85**
J	**85**
K	**91**
L	**95**
M	**101**
N	**111**
O	**115**
P	**118**
R	**126**
S	**136**
T	**150**
U	**161**
V	**161**
W	**164**
Y	**174**
BIBLIOGRAPHY	**175**
INDEX of people without individual entries	**177**

LIST OF ILLUSTRATIONS

	Page
Olave Baden-Powell	18
Aubrey Beardsley	18
Sir Donald Bailey	18
Archibald Beckett	27
Morden Bennett	27
Mary Broad	27
Holy Trinity Church	28
Frederick Bright's Store	28
The Gardens	28
Boscombe Manor (Grovely Manor School)	38
Southbourne Pier	38
Christopher Crabbe Creeke	45
Joseph Cutler	45
Sir Henry Drummond Wolff	51
Mont Dore Hotel	51
Edward VII arriving at the Royal Victoria Hospital	54
Bournemouth West Station	54
Empress Elizabeth of Austria	59
Winter Gardens	59
The Bath Hotel	62
The East Cliff Hall	62
Sir Dan Godfrey's Band	71
The Shelley Tomb	71
Highcliff Hotel	72
East Cliff Cottage Hotel	72
Thomas Hankinson	76
Marguerite Radclyffe Hall	76
Thomas Hardy	76
Sir Henry Irving	84
South Bourne Terrace	84
John Keble	90
Brookside	90
Lillie Langtry	94
Boscombe Arcade	97
The Lodge, Talbot Woods	97

LIST OF ILLUSTRATIONS (continued)

	Page
The 1st Earl of Malmesbury	103
The 3rd Earl of Malmesbury	103
Brusher Mills	108
Hinton Admiral	108
VC Holders Plaque	113
Stewart's Hotel	113
Robert Old	117
Oscar II, King of Sweden with Queen Sofia	117
1st Viscount Portman	121
Portman Lodge	121
Sir Henry Page Croft	125
William Morley Punshon	125
William Rebbeck	128
Foxholes	128
Henry Robson	131
John Roberts Thomson	131
Charles Rolls	131
Sir Merton Russell-Côtes	134
Gordon Selfridge	139
Sir Percy Shelley	139
Robert Southey	145
Robert Louis Stevenson	145
Ken Sprague	145
John Sydenham's Reading Room	149
Count Vladimir Tchertkov's printing press	153
Lewis Tregonwell	158
Paul Verlaine	162
Baroness Pauline von Hügel	162
The Osborne, Exeter Road	166
Beatrice Webb	166
Oscar Wilde	170
Chang Woo Gow	170

ABOUT THE AUTHOR

Leigh Hatts was born in Bournemouth and is a member of the Bournemouth Civic Society. He is the author of *Poole & Sandbanks: Photographic Memories*, which he wrote with his wife Marion Marples, and *Exploring The Bournemouth Coast Path*. His other books include *The Thames Path*, *The Lea Valley Walk* and *London City Churches*.

He is the son of the late Kenneth Hatts, whose drawing of Beatrice Webb is included in this book, and recalls hearing his grandmother speaking about her life in Bournemouth early in the 20th century.

FOREWORD

This book is written as a contribution to Bournemouth's bi-centenary celebrations in 2010.

The town takes 1810 as its foundation year for that is when Lewis Tregonwell brought his wife Henrietta to see the Bourne stream running into the sea. She so loved the spot they decided to build a house.

There were already one or two buildings within the boundary of the future borough including an inn at 'Bourne', a Georgian house at Southbourne and a Saxon church at Holdenhurst. But Tregonwell's new house marked the start of development.

The first known visitor after this event was a friend of the poet Shelley whose own heart was to eventually rest in Bournemouth. This book highlights just some of the famous who have visited or lived in Bournemouth and a few of those who became well-known within the town for their pioneering work.

I have included information about personalities not recorded elsewhere which is why some people have longer entries than others who may be better known.

My thanks for patience and help go to Bournemouth Library's Heritage Zone, The London Library, Dr Williams' Library and The Women's Library at London Metropolitan University.

I also wish to thank Alan J Miller, author of *Old Bournemouth: the Story of the Bourne Tregonwell Estate*, for helping to confirm that the first visit of Tregonwell and his wife was 14 June 1810 rather than the often quoted date of 14 July.

I am most grateful to Bournemouth-born Ian A Taylor, local Fabian Society secretary for forty years, Bournemouth historian John Walker and my Poole-born wife Marion Marples who all read the draft text and offered advice.

I hope this book will jog memories. Those with new information could post it on the accompanying website www.bournemouthpeople.com or write to me c/o Natula Publications.

Leigh Hatts, May 2010

PLACES FREQUENTLY MENTIONED

BIC: Bournemouth International Centre was built in Exeter Road for conferences and entertainment and opened in 1984.

Blacklock's Pharmacy was at 14 Commercial Road (now Miss Selfridge).

Boscombe Hippodrome opened in 1890 as the Grand Pavilion Theatre and took the new name in 1905. It has also been known as the Boscombe Ballrooms, the Opera House and is now called the O2 Academy Bournemouth. It stands alongside Boscombe Arcade.

Boscombe Manor: see Shelley Park.

Bournemouth East Station: see Bournemouth Station.

Bournemouth High School was in Surrey Road and has been called Talbot Heath since it moved in 1935 to its present site.

Bournemouth (Municipal) College of Art: see Drummond Road Art School.

Bournemouth & Poole College of Art: see Drummond Road Art School.

Bournemouth Station opened on 20 July 1885 as Bournemouth East Station and was renamed Bournemouth Central on 1 May 1899. It became Bournemouth Station in 1969 after Bournemouth West closed. The original Bournemouth East Station was on the east side of Holdenhurst Road.

Bournemouth School of Art: see Drummond Road Art School.

Bournemouth School for Boys was founded in 1901 in Porchester Road and moved to its present site in East Way in 1940. The original building became Porchester School and has now been replaced by Fenwick Court.

Commissioner: The Commissioners of the Bournemouth Improvement District were formed following the Bournemouth Improvement Act 1856 and were the forerunner of Bournemouth Council which dates from 1890 borough status.

Drummond Road Art School was at 58 Drummond Road (since demolished) opposite Hengist Road. This was the forerunner of the Bournemouth School of Art which opened at The Lansdowne in 1913 and was later called the Bourne-mouth College of Art and now the Bournemouth & Poole College of Art.

East Cliff Hall is now the Russell-Côtes Art Gallery & Museum.

Grand Theatre, Boscombe: see Boscombe Hippodrome.

Grovely Manor School occupied Shelley Park from 1911 to 1938.

Hahnemann House: The Hahnemann Convalescent Home & Homoeopathic Dispensary in Hahnemann Road opened in 1897 and is now part of the NHS.

Holy Trinity Church was built in 1869 on the eastern corner of Lorne Park Road/Old Christchurch Road junction. The church was demolished in 1979.

Horace G Commin, bookshop at 100 Old Christchurch Road is now Enigma.

Labour Hall: see Lincoln Hall.

Lincoln Hall, built as Labour Hall in Lincoln Avenue, has been replaced by flats.

Palace Court Hotel, Westover Road is now Premier Lodge.

Palace Court Theatre, Hinton Road is now the Wessex Christian Centre.

Portman Lodge was built in about 1811 for Louis Tregonwell* as his butler's home and stood on the east side of Exeter Road, opposite Cranborne Road. The Tregonwells soon preferred this thatched cottage to The Mansion. Portman Lodge was destroyed by fire in 1922.

Richmond Hill Congregational Church is now St Andrew's United Reform Church. The original church was demolished and the current building erected on the site in 1891.

Saugeen School was on site of the Majestic Hotel in Derby Road from 1873 to 1935.

Shelley Park was also known as Boscombe Cottage and Boscombe Manor; see Grovely Manor.

Skerryvore: RL Stevenson's house in Alum Chine Road, hit by a bomb in the Second World War, and now a public garden.

Theatre Royal, designed by Kemp-Welch & Pinder, opened in 1882 in Albert Road where the building survives.

The Knole, Knole Road: Now a Masonic property.

Westbourne Hospital also known as Westbourne Eye Hospital, was the Royal Victoria Hospital (now flats), on west corner of Poole Road/Clarendon Road junction.

Winter Gardens was a glass hall, like a small Crystal Palace, built in 1877 and replaced in 1937 by a brick building which was recently demolished.

Wychwood School started at Wychwood 53 Wellington Road in 1898 and moved to the Ladycross (now Wychwood Close) in Braidley Road in 1905. The house had been purpose built a decade earlier for England's first Roman Catholic preparatory school. Wychwood boys were a familiar sight in their knickerbockers. Howard Thomas was headmaster from 1938 until the school closed in 1966.

NOTES ON THE TEXT

Mention of any of the above places in the text are indicated by the use of the ^ symbol; an asterisk after a name (such as Charles Darwin*) indicates that he or she has an individual entry.

A

ABBERLINE, Frederick (1843-1929), detective involved in 1888 'Jack the Ripper' hunt and in charge of the Cleveland Street scandal investigation, retired to Bournemouth in 1904 living first at 4 Methuen Road (demolished for Wessex Way) and finally from 1911 at Estcourt 195 Holdenhurst Road where there is a blue plaque. He is buried in the Wimborne Road Cemetery and has been depicted in films by Michael Caine and Johnny Depp.

ABINGER, 5th Lord (1872-1917), PB Shelley* heir. The poet's childless son Sir Percy Shelley* and his wife Jane* adopted her niece Florence Gibson who in 1871 married Captain Leopold Scarlett, the future Lord Abinger, at Christchurch Priory Church. Their son Shelley Leopold Lawrence was born at Boscombe Manor^ the following year. When widowed Lady Shelley died in 1899 he inherited the house and two months later he married Lila Lucy White at Corpus Christi Church in Boscombe. In 1903 he succeeded his cousin as the 5th Lord Abinger and lived at Boscombe Manor. They supported Boscombe Hospital by holding garden parties, sending flowers from the garden and supplying pheasants at Christmas. In 1911 Lord Abinger sold the property. In 1979 the 8th Baron Abinger visited Shelley Park^ to open the short-lived Shelley Rooms museum.

ALLINGHAM, William (1824-1889), poet, visited Boscombe when living at Lymington. In October 1864, whilst on his way from Christchurch to stay in Bournemouth, he left his card and a letter of introduction from Lord Houghton at Boscombe Manor^ lodge (which stood at the north end of the drive now known as Chessel Avenue). After lunch he walked back to Boscombe and called on Lady Shelley* who invited him to join her and Sir Percy Shelley* for dinner the following night, Saturday 29 October. At the meal he found himself sitting between the poet's two surviving sisters. One, Hellen Shelley, wore a light purple silk dress with white satin shoes. Another guest was Grantley Berkeley*.

Four years later Allingham was invited to lunch at Boscombe in early December. Afterwards Sir Percy walked with him half way to Christchurch where there was the nearest station. The following weekend Sir Percy's steamship *Nökken* called at Lymington to take Allingham on a cruise round the Isle of Wight.

ANDERTON, William (1816-1890), priest and novelist. After being secretary to his uncle Cardinal Henry Manning, when appointed Archbishop of Westminster, Anderton joined the Jesuits and spent a year (c1876) at the Sacred Heart Church. Among visitors to the Presbytery in Albert Road was Paul Verlaine* whilst the congregation included Raphael Merry del Val*.

ARGYLL, 8th Duke of (1823-1900) came to Bournemouth in 1846 by way of Winchester which was then the nearest railway station. He visited for his health and walked among pines on the East Cliff. Later, when staying at the (Royal) Bath Hotel, he advised Merton Russell-Côtes* that investment in the hotel would have a return. In 1889 the Duke opened Boscombe Pier. Argyll Road is named after him.

ARNOLD, Malcolm (1921-2006), composer, was inspired to be a trumpet player when as a boy he met Louis Armstrong at the Royal Bath Hotel. Many years later when Arnold returned to conduct the Bournemouth Symphony Orchestra he was said to be found afterwards in a pub playing a piano. His Second Symphony had its première at the Winter Gardens^ in May 1952 when Charles Groves* conducted the work. Groves was later to champion the Ninth Symphony after it had waited six years for its first performance.

ARNOLD, Matthew (1822-1888), poet and son of Dr Thomas Arnold, visited Bournemouth in 1849 and afterwards wrote in a letter: "...in Bournemouth by the Sea, a great moorland covered with furze and low pine woods comes down to the sea shore, and breaks down towards it in a long sweep of cliff, half sand, half mud." He added: "...to the right and left you see one immense, gradually curving line till the coast ends in two ordinary headlands at great distances on each side." He described the Bourne as "a little brook". His godfather was John Keble* who later lived in a house overlooking the stream.

ATTLEE, Clement (1883-1967), Prime Minister, opened the 1937 Labour Party Conference at The Pavilion by speaking warmly of Bournemouth's municipal enterprises on the seafront and suggesting that the motive of service replacing profit could be applied nationwide. "There is a beauty in Bournemouth," the Opposition Leader said. "We want a beautiful Britain - a place where men, women and children can lead fine lives."

The weather was sunny in May 1940 as the Labour Conference delegates arrived in the town. After a National Executive meeting in the Highcliff Hotel basement, Attlee told Downing Street by telephone from the hotel's front desk that Labour would only join a coalition under "another Prime Minister". As a result, premier Neville Chamberlain resigned immediately and Churchill was invited by George VI to form the war coalition government.

During his retirement, Attlee stayed at the Imperial Hotel (Roundhouse Hotel site at The Lansdowne) in 1962 and rested in a deckchair with rug over his knees on the Pier.

Olave Baden-Powell

Aubrey Beardsley
Memorial, Exeter Road, Bournemouth

Sir Donald Bailey, memorial plaque in Christchurch Priory Church

B

BADDELEY, William (1914-1998), Dean of Brisbane, was curate at St Stephen's Church from 1946 to 1949.

BADEN-POWELL, Olave (1889-1977), Chief Guide and wife of Sir Robert Baden-Powell. In 1900 the 11 year old spent eight weeks in a Bournemouth hotel with her parents. One outing was to the Winter Gardens^ to see a Shakespeare play. Afterwards the family rented Cranborne Manor. In 1908, the year after the Scout movement was founded on Brownsea Island, the family moved to Lilliput. One a day a week she taught at the Invalid Children's Aid Association home in Bournemouth. At the age of 23 she married Robert Baden-Powell at St Peter's Church, Parkstone.

BAILEY, Sir Donald (1901-1985), Bailey Bridge inventor, lived at 14 Viking Close at Southbourne. In 1973 he stayed at Strathallan Nursing Home for a while but in 1979, at the age of 77, he married his former housekeeper Mildred Stacey at St Nicholas Church, Hengistbury Head. To mark his 80th birthday in 1981 the Mary Ford Cake Artistry Centre at Southbourne made a cake in the shape of a Bailey Bridge.

BAILY, Ken (1911-1993), England Cheerleader who came from Glastonbury at the age of 27 with his mother and lived in the same flat at Queensbury Mansions in Parsonage Road until his death. In 1939 he ran in a relay from Southampton to New York by running round the deck of a moving liner. With others he was carrying a torch to appeal to Roosevelt to support the Allies in the coming Second World War. In 1948 he carried the London Olympic flame. For many years he ran with a torch from the Highcliff Hotel to the Pier during Regatta Week to start the fireworks display.

As the English Football Supporters Association standard bearer he travelled all over the country and abroad dressed as John Bull and become the unofficial World Cup cheerleader. In Australia he was spotted in a crowd by the Queen who said to the Mayor of Sydney "Look who's here!" In Bournemouth he met Prince Charles as he arrived at The Pavilion for a union conference and some years later greeted his wife the Princess of Wales.

In 1982 at half-time during the England v Australia rugby match at Twickenham he rushed on to the field to cover the 24 year old streaker Erica Roe with his Union Jack.

He was a daily sea swimmer and for many years wrote the Genevieve society column in the *Bournemouth Times* which made him well-known in the town before his national fame.

He worked at Telephone House 18 Christchurch Road and briefly for Beales store before inheriting some money. In 1976 he was made a freeman of Bournemouth and is buried at the entrance to Wimborne Road Cemetery.

BALDWIN, Stanley (1867-1947), Prime Minister, addressed the Conservative Conference at The Pavilion on 3 October 1935 foretelling the coming General Election which he announced on 19 October. This elected the Parliament which sat for ten years due to the Second World War.

BALFOUR, Kenneth (1863-1936), owner of Brownsea Island (1891-1901) and MP for Christchurch which included Bournemouth (1900-1906). He stood as a Conservative and defeated his Liberal opponent TH Brassey by just three votes. He lived in Dorset and died by chance in his former constituency having been admitted to Stagden Nursing Home (since demolished) 16 West Cliff Road. He was buried in the family plot in Bournemouth Cemetery.

BASSET, Bernard (1909-1988), well-known and influential Jesuit priest. The years from 1962 to 1969 were his most prolific as an author and witty preacher. His home base was the Sacred Heart Church presbytery in Albert Road where his brother Edmund was the parish priest.

BATH, Peter (1927-2006), travel agent and ABTA founder member. Bath Travel was started in 1924 by his father Reginald at the present 2 Albert Road address. After serving in the Royal Navy during the Second World War, he joined the family firm as office boy. In 1950 he married a nurse Elizabeth Moss who he had met at St Katharine's youth club. Seven years later his father died leaving him in sole charge and gradually he opened more than fifty branches in the south of England. In 1958 he started Palmair which ran tours from Bournemouth to Majorca and in 1993 launched an airline which by the time of his death had two jets operating from Bournemouth Airport. He was present at every departure to personally greet and wave off the passengers who, on board, enjoyed plenty of leg room and refreshments. In 2003 Palmair was voted the Britain's favourite airline by *Which?* magazine. He was awarded the MBE in 2005.

His own holidays were spent in a beach hut on Mudeford Sandspit. In 1992 he handed over management of the business to his children.

BATTENBERG, Prince Henry (1858-1896), husband of Queen Victoria's daughter Beatrice*. In 1895, just months before his sudden death, he travelled to Bournemouth to visit the Royal Counties Agricultural Show in the grounds of Littledown House (now JP Morgan) near Castle Lane. After being driven along a decorated route from the station to the Royal Bath Hotel he was amazed to see six beefeaters at the entrance and asked owner Sir Merton Russell-Côtes* how he had managed to obtain their services. Sir Merton had to confess that the men were locals dressed in hired costumes. The prince attended the Society's dinner at the hotel and stayed the night. After breakfast he planted a tree in the garden before visiting Meyrick Park golf course.

BAYLIS, Thomas (1817-1908), lawyer who wrote *The Rights, Duties, and Relations of Domestic Servants and their Masters and Mistresses* (1857), died at Lucknow (now Beechwood House) on the corner of Beechey and Wellington Roads and was buried in Bournemouth Cemetery.

BAYLY, Samuel (1798-1864), first hotel owner, was a draper in Christchurch who lived in nearby Purewell where he had built Hengistbury House. In 1838 he leased land on the east bank of the Bourne Stream at the bottom of Bath Hill from St George Meyrick* and opened the Belle Vue Boarding House. This soon became the focal point of the growing community. In 1848 John Sydenham* opened a single storey reading room in an attached building alongside the stream. An Assembly Rooms, designed by Christopher Crabbe Creek* and built behind in 1855, was used for dinners and meetings. Congregational and Roman Catholic Church services were held there and in 1910 it became a synagogue. The buildings were demolished in 1924 to make way for The Pavilion. In 1856 Bayly was one of the town's first Commissioners but was disqualified by non-attendance at meetings. The following year he went bankrupt and the building was sold although it continued as the Belle Vue & Pier Hotel.

BEALE, John Elmes (1848-1928), founder of Beales, opened Beale Fancy Fair on the present Beales site in December 1881. In 1885 the shop, by now called JE Beale and with the upper floor devoted to German toys, was the first in Britain to have Father Christmas in residence. The very realistic costumed figure always had his head uncovered as Beale's wife Annie found making a hood for her brother Ernest too difficult. Father Christmas, who in 1912 arrived in Meyrick Park on a Wright Brothers plane, last visited in 1997.

Beale was Mayor of Bournemouth from 1902 to 1904 when he welcomed Princess Louise* to Westbourne Hospital^. He was partly responsible for JD Jones* being appointed minister of Richmond Hill Congregational Church^ and later both men with their wives toured the USA together. Beale slowly bought up the neighbouring shops and continued to expand even after erecting a purpose built store in 1905; another rebuild followed in 1912. He lived at Bridgend (Queensbury Mansions site) in Parsonage Road. His son Bennett was Mayor and another son Herbert married Miss Tyrell of the rival store Plummer Roddis & Tyrell. The Beale memorial window is in St Andrew's United Reformed Church where as a Congregationalist he worshipped.

BEARDSLEY, Aubrey (1872-1898), artist, suffering from tuberculosis, arrived in Boscombe in August 1896 to stay at Pier View boarding house (site of The Point flats at the junction of Sea Road and The Marina). As he worked in his upstairs room, at a table facing the sea, he was flanked by his own two ormolu candlesticks which slightly resembled the two depicted on a dressing table in his 1894 drawing La Dame aux Camélias for *The Yellow Book*. He also brought two Chippendale settees.

At first both his mother Ellen and his actress sister Mable were with him. His first visitor was erotic writer and publisher Leonard Smithers who paid him a weekly cheque and raised his spirits by suggesting an album of past work. Beardsley started writing to publishers for permission reproduce his best drawings but a visit to London at the end of the month to see publishers affected his health.

He worked, often in bed, producing a binding-block design as well as drawings for friends. He also provided cover designs for the magazine *The Savoy* but its publication was ceased by Smithers at the end of the year. Beardsley's association with the magazine was not good for sales as he was seen to have been not only too close to the disgraced Oscar Wilde* but a producer of highly erotic drawings. WH Smith refused to stock the magazine. The November issue of the *Magazine of Art* carried an article called 'Aubrey Beardsley and Decadents'.

However, he wrote a poem for the penultimate issue of *The Savoy* and was pleased to win the approval of poet John Gray. Art patron Marc-André Raffalovich was in constant touch sending chocolates, flowers and books. Beardsley had managed at least once to visit Corpus Christi Church at Boscombe and early in November Father Charles de Lapasture called on him. About this time the American Roman Catholic writer Vincent O'Sullivan, who was staying in Bournemouth, called. Beardsley had earlier been working on a frontispiece for his short stories. He was also friendly with Eleanor Towle (Taylor*), wife of the Vicar of St Clements Church.

He produced five drawings for a play *The Pierrot of the Minute* but was plagued by toothache and had an extraction at the dentist in Christchurch Road on the western corner (now demolished) of Hamilton Road.

In December he suffered a haemorrhage near the top of the path to the East Cliff. On his struggle back to the hotel with his sister he drank some spa water from the thatched hut at the Boscombe Chine entrance.

On Christmas Day residents and guests placed small presents by his breakfast place. He was too ill to go to church and after lunch took to his bed feeling very low.

In the New Year he was caught up in the excitement caused by the discovery of a 65 foot long whale washed up on the beach east of Boscombe Pier. A change of scene was suggested and Horace G Commin^ came to pack his books. At the end of January he moved with his mother to Bournemouth where he took up residence in furnished rooms at Muriel, a house (since demolished and its site marked by a mosaic of a Beardsley drawing) next to St Andrew's Church (now a nightclub) in Exeter Road. Opposite was the thatched Portman Lodge^.

Muriel was a corner house built by Joseph Cutler* in 1871 with three front doors on different levels in Exeter Road and Terrace Road.

Here he began using watercolour for a drawing *Mademoiselle de Maupin*. *The Book of Fifty Drawings*, suggested by Smithers in the summer, came out in January and received a poor review in *The Daily Telegraph* although Max Beerbolm was enthusiastic in *Tomorrow*.

Gray and Raffalovich came for a few days around 16 February. The latter arranged for Father David Bearne from the Sacred Heart Church to visit. When he was well enough, Beardsley attended the church. At the end of the month Jerome Pollitt visited and received the bookplate he had ordered two years earlier. Smithers came next and had his photograph taken with Beardsley and his mother by local photographer WJ Hawker, a friend of impresario Charles Cochran who had been at school with Beardsley.

In March confidence about his health improved after he had attended a concert at the Winter Gardens^ with Dr JD Harsant, his Bournemouth doctor who lived nearby at The Hive (Punshon site). Despite often feeling tired Beardsley continued working. He visited the Sacred Heart on Friday 26 March but on the following Wednesday he was too ill to go to again and Father Bearne came to the house to receive him into the Roman Catholic Church. Beardsley wrote to tell Raffalovich the good news and on Friday made his first communion at home. On Dr Harsant's recommendation he left Bournemouth by train on Friday 9 April for London on his way to Menton on the French Riviera where he died the following year.

BEATLES, The: the four-strong pop group. Paul McCartney, George Harrison, Ringo Starr and John Lennon appeared on stage at the Gaumont (now the Odeon) in Westover Road for a week in August 1963 as "Britain's fabulous disc stars The Beatles" with Billy J Kramer as the support act. It was the week when the Beatles' *She Loves You* record was released. Around 600 people queued all day and all night for tickets. With a supporting cast, the four only played for twenty minutes at each performance. They arrived early in a police van at the back of the cinema to avoid the fans. Police were on duty inside the theatre. During the week George Harrison wrote the song *Don't Bother Me* which was later included in the *With The Beatles* album. They returned on Saturday 16 November for two evening shows at the Winter Gardens^ which were recorded for USA television and provided Americans with their introduction to the band. However, coverage was not as extensive as intended. Transmission was set for a week later on 22 November, the day President John Kennedy was assassinated.

In 1964 they appeared at the Gaumont on 2 August and 30 October. The year after John Lennon bought his aunt Mimi a bungalow at Sandbanks.

The cover image of the Beatles second album *With The Beatles* was taken on 22 August 1963 at the nearby Palace Court Hotel^ (now the Premier Lodge) where the group was staying. The photographer was Robert Freeman who placed the Beatles in a corridor where a window lit the four from one side. In 2007 this picture was used on a commemorative postage stamp. The group also posed on the hotel roof with the West Cliff and Isle of Purbeck across the bay as a backdrop. Harry Taylor* took many photographs during the visits including one of the four eating rock.

BEATRICE, Princess (1857-1944), daughter of Queen Victoria and wife of Prince Henry of Battenberg*, opened the Russell-Côtes Art Gallery & Museum in the presence of Sir Merton Russell-Côtes* and his wife at East Cliff Hall^ in 1919.

BECKETT, Archibald (1842-1904), early promoter of Boscombe as a destination, was responsible for the building of Boscombe Arcade, the adjacent ballrooms (O2 Academy Bournemouth) on the east side and 35-bedroom Salisbury Hotel (now a McDonalds site) on the corner of Palmerston Road between 1890 and 1895. The arcade was opened as the Grand Continental Arcade in 1893 by the Duke of Connaught* whilst the ballroom, opened in 1895, was called the Grand Pavilion Theatre. The architect and contractor was Lawson* & Donkin. Concerts were given several times a day from the first floor stage in the arcade. Performers included the Boscombe Band sponsored by Beckett. So popular was the complex that a dinner was held in his honour when he received a gold watch inscribed 'Presented to Archibald Beckett by a few friends as a tribute to his indefatigable energy for the good of Boscombe.'

Beckett was a Boscombe councillor who was soon involved in an audacious attempt to build shops and houses below the East Cliff until thwarted by the Council which built the promenade. By 1898 Beckett had sold his interest in both the arcade and the hotel.

BELSKY, Margaret (1919-1989), cartoonist known as 'Belsky'. Her work appeared in many publications including *The Daily Herald* in the 1950s, when she was the only woman daily cartoonist, and also in *The Guardian*. Margaret Owen, whilst at Bournemouth School of Art^, won a *Punch* competition and a place at the Royal College of Art where she met her husband sculptor Franta Belsky.

BENNETT, (Alexander) Morden (1808-1880), Vicar of St Peter's Church for 35 years. When appointed Perpetual Curate (vicar) of St Peter's in 1845 he was assistant priest at London's Portman Chapel in Baker Street, a church influenced by the Oxford Movement. Its chaplain was the controversial William Bennett who in 1850 founded the Anglo-Catholic St Barnabas, Pimlico. It was this emerging Tractarian tradition that Bennett brought to Bournemouth. He was the first priest in the Winchester Diocese since the Reformation to introduce a daily Eucharist. Five years later a visitor said: "Puseyism flourished like the rhododendrons." For five winter months in 1865-6 the congregation included John Keble*.

Bennett was just married to his second wife Marianne Hopkins of Christchurch who may have encouraged him to move to Bournemouth. He arrived for his first Sunday having ridden from Mudeford and left his horse at the Belle Vue Hotel (Pier Approach site). The family moved into the new Vicarage (Bath Hill Court site) in Parsonage Road the following year. One of his early baptisms was Hubert Parry*.

Bennett presided over a massive expansion of the Church of England mission in the growing town. The churches: St Ambrose at Westbourne, St Clement's on the edge of Boscombe, St James's at Pokesdown, St John's Moordown, St Michael's on Poole Hill and St Swithun's in Manor Road all opened as a result of his energy and awareness that some people perceived St

Peter's Church to be too far and too rich. He was even responsible for St Barnabas Church at East Parley, reached by the Redhill ferry, and for encouraging the building of All Saints Church in Branksome Park which fell in the neighbouring diocese. Some of the churches were designed by George Edmund Street* who collaborated with Bennett to rebuild St Peter's Church on a scale which would serve the rising population. The service of thanksgiving for the completion of the mother church took place on 18 December 1879, just a month before Bennett's death. His memorial is in St Stephen's Church where his son Alexander Sykes was the first vicar.

BENNETT, Charles (1870-1948), Britain's first Olympic gold medal winner, took part in 1900 Paris Games as a runner coming first in the 500 metres and went on to win another gold and a silver medal. At the time he was an engine driver living at Shapwick near Wimborne but soon after became landlord of The Dolphin (now Gulliver's Tavern) in Kinson. Later he lived at Holt Lodge in Wimborne Road. He is buried in Kinson churchyard.

BERINGER, Oscar (1844-1922), composer and pianist. In the 1870s, having founded the Academy for the Higher Development of Piano Forte Playing in London, he taught piano at Stirling House School at the top of Bath Road where Beatrice Webb* was a pupil.

BERKELEY, Grantley (1800-1881), colourful politician and sportsman, who claimed to have witnessed Sir George Tapps* ordering the planting of the first pines. Berkeley was a regular guest at the theatrical performances at the home of Sir Percy Shelley* and even expressed a desire to write a play called *A Trip to Bournemouth*.

BERLIN, Irving (1888-1989), American composer, brought his wartime show *This Is the Army* to the Boscombe Hippodrome^ for a week in January 1940. The 160 strong cast was backed by an orchestra of thirty which arrived on a special train. Profits went to war charities and half the theatre seats were available free to members of the armed services. Songs sung by Berlin in the show included *Oh How I Hate To Get Up In The Morning* and *White Christmas*. Although he was shocked by the effect bombing had, he still thought Bournemouth was the most beautiful British town he had visited.

BERNADOTTE, Prince of Sweden (Oscar; Count of Wisborg from 1892) (1859-1953), second son of King Oscar II* of Sweden and Norway and younger brother of King Gustav V, was married at St Stephen's Church in

Archibald Beckett

Morden Bennett and St Stephen's Church

Mary Broad

Holy Trinity Church

Sir Anthony Blunt was born when his father was the vicar.

Frederick Bright's store

North Front, The Arcade, Old Christchurch Road

The Gardens. Some paths and shrubbery were laid out by Decimus Burton

1888. His bride was commoner Ebba Munck. Present were Queen Sofia* of Sweden and Norway, the Crown Princess of Denmark (who visited the town the year before) and the Duchess of Albany, daughter of Queen Victoria.

The bride, a former maid of honour to the Crown Princess, had earlier called off an engagement to a soldier. Prince Oscar, a naval officer, returned from two year voyage round the world and fell in love with Ebba. Although she loved the Prince, Ebba was aware that marriage would deprive him of his rights and privileges. Despite her feelings she at once left the Swedish court to avoid him and worked in a hospital. She only confessed her love for him and yielded when the Prince told her that the Queen had given her consent. Eventually the King also gave his to please his wife who was due to have an operation.

The bridegroom was dressed in the uniform of a Swedish Navy captain and his bride wore white with a crown of myrtle. But for the death of the Kaiser a few days earlier it would have been a much grander occasion.

The Lutheran ceremony, presided over by a Royal chaplain, was the first wedding in the church which had been in use for just three years with only the nave and aisles completed. Queen Sofia donated £60 to the building fund.

The Prince, who by marriage lost his right of succession to the throne on the same day, adopted the title Prince Bernadotte. The couple's son, UN peace envoy Count Folke Bernadotte, was assassinated in 1948.

BERNHARDT, Sarah (1844-1923), actress, took tea with Sir Merton and Lady Russell-Côtes* at East Cliff Hall^ where she admired the art collection and especially the Japanese items. She was appearing at the Boscombe Hippodrome^ at the time.

BEST, George (1946-2005), international footballer, played for Bournemouth Football Club just five times during the 1983 season in his last competitive league games.

BEST, Rayleigh Breton Amis (1905-1972), author, moved in 1939 to 11 Victoria Avenue and contributed to magazines. He wrote novels under the names Rayleigh Best and Breton Amis, contributing to the *Yarrow Series*. He based *Park Royal*, published in 1950 and featuring a seaside council, on Bournemouth.

BETJEMAN, Sir John (1906-1984), Poet Laureate and Founding President of the Bournemouth Civic Society, described Bournemouth as a "stately Victorian duchess". St Stephen's Church was "the most beautiful Victorian church in the south-west" and "worth travelling 200 miles and being sick in the coach to have seen inside this many vistaed church, all in cream-coloured stone, with arch cutting arch, a lofty hall of stone vaulting providing view after view as you walk round it, each lovelier than the next and worthy of a vast cathedral". The draft opening of his poem *Goodbye* was written on the flap of his one inch Bournemouth Ordnance Survey map. He was a speaker in the Bournemouth Arts Club's *Art in Our Time* Series.

BLUNT, Sir Anthony (1907-1973), art historian and spy, was born at the Holy Trinity Vicarage (Benjamin Court site) in Madeira Road. His father Stanley was Vicar of Holy Trinity Church^ from 1906. At the time he already had two sons, Wilfred the future art curator and Christopher who became an expert on British coinage. Anthony was a toddler in 1910 when his grandfather Bishop RFL Blunt died at the Vicarage. The family left Bournemouth in 1912 when his father was appointed chaplain to the British Embassy Church in Paris. After the Second World War, having become Surveyor of the Queen's Pictures but not yet unmasked as a Russian spy, Anthony was a speaker in the Bournemouth Arts Club's *Art in Our Time* Series.

BODLEY, GF (1827-1907), architect and uncle of Thomas Bodley Scott*. His work included the ceiling of St Peter's Church in Bournemouth. Towards the end of his life he designed St Aldhelm's Church, Branksome Park. Its plain exterior is due to a failure to complete Bodley's plan which included a tower and cloister-style arcade.

BODLEY SCOTT, Sir Ronald (1906-1982), Physician to Elizabeth II from her accession in 1952 until 1982, was born in Bournemouth, son of Dr Maitland Scott and his wife Alice. He was a grandson of Dr Thomas Bodley Scott* and joined the family practice at 11 Poole Road from St Bartholomew's Hospital but was soon persuaded to return to London.

BODLEY SCOTT, Thomas (1851-1924), doctor, mayor, nephew of architects GF Bodley* and Sir George Gilbert Scott and, through his mother Georgina, a descendant of Sir Thomas Bodley, founder of Oxford's Bodleian Library. From 1876 Thomas Bodley Scott and his wife Adeline lived at Aldington, 7 Poole Road (now Poole Road Medical Centre). The doctor was a general practitioner and his patients included Robert Louis Stevenson*. Lady Shelley* claimed that it was Dr Bodley Scott's prescription of Indian hemp for curing haemorrhages that caused the fevered dreams which resulted in Stevenson writing *The Strange Case of Dr Jekyll and Mr Hyde*. Stevenson dedicated his collection of poems *Underwoods* to his doctor.

Bodley Scott was the first doctor to attend Winston Churchill* when he fell from the bridge. His novel *The Inside of the Cup* had a great influence on the doctor who was interested in effects of the Christian faith.

Bodley Scott's own books included *The Road to a Healthy Old Age* which ran to several editions, *Why Do We Die?* and *Endocrine Therapeutics*. In 1919 he planned to write a biography of Sir Lauder Brunton who established a link between blood pressure and angina.

But on his retirement in 1921 Bodley Scott was elected councillor for his own West Cliff Ward. As mayor in 1923 he quoted Stevenson in his acceptance speech: "...to travel hopefully is a better thing than to arrive". The doctor served for just over three months before sudden death. His funeral was at St Michael's Church which he had attended for over fifty years and where the tower was designed by his relative John Oldrid Scott.

His grandson was Sir Ronald Bodley Scott*.

BOOTHBY, Guy (1867-1905), horror and science fiction writer, came to live in the Bournemouth area soon after his marriage to Rose in 1895. They lived at first in Parsonage Road and then brought up their family of two daughters and a son just outside the town where they bred horses, cattle and dogs. Having written his Dr Nikola series of books, he moved to Winsley Lodge in Watkin Road at Boscombe. After his unexpected death there from flu he was buried at Bournemouth Cemetery where the service was conducted by SC Lowry*.

BOTT, Edmund (1740-1788), son of the 'divine' Thomas Bott and lawyer, built Stourfield House (Douglas Mews site in Southbourne) in 1766 after leaving London due to poor health. He became a JP and in 1771 published *Statutes and Decisions Respecting the Poor Laws*. He was often called upon to confirm assessments of the Christchurch poor before they received relief. He is buried in the Lady Chapel at Christchurch Priory Church. After his death, Stourfield House was the home of the Countess of Strathmore*.

BRACKEN, Brendan (1901-1958), Second World War cabinet minister and later Bournemouth MP who was Evelyn Waugh's inspiration for Rex Mottram in *Brideshead Revisited*. In 1945 he was imposed as Conservative candidate after Churchill had raised the sitting member Sir Leonard Lyle* to the peerage. Bracken's opponents at the election were Edward Shackleton* (Labour), who polled over 16,000 votes, and Basil Wigoder (Liberal), the lawyer and future peer.

As MP, Bracken was assiduous in visiting the town at weekends when he dined at Sweeting's Restaurant 86 Old Christchurch Road (now Ashes) or The Carlton Hotel where he enjoyed the sea view. But he never, despite stated intentions, had a home in the constituency. However, his half sister Cara moved to the town as did his brother Peter with whom he had a difficult relationship.

In 1950, when the constituency was split, Bracken chose to be candidate for Bournemouth East & Christchurch where he won a large majority against the Labour candidate Dodo Lees*. In 1952 his Commons career was cut short when he was forced to accept a peerage from his patron Churchill. Bracken reluctantly became Lord Bracken of Christchurch but never took his seat in the Lords. His memorial is Bracken House, the former headquarters of *The Financial Times*, in London.

BRAZIL, Angela (1868-1947), children's writer who produced almost fifty books mostly with a school setting. She based characters in *A Patriotic Schoolgirl* (1918) on her sister-in-law Florence and nephew Jack who lived on the top floor above a shop at 19a St Catherine's Road at Southbourne.

BRIGHT, Frederick (1832-1905), founder of Bright's department store, opened his needlework and wool shop in the still roofless five year old Arcade in 1871. The former missionary from Essex and his Swanage-born wife had a son Percy who was born at Mirzapore in India when Frederick was working for the London Missionary Society. On returning to England he went briefly to Poole and then ran a shop for six years in Lymington before moving along the coast. As Bright & Son, the Bournemouth shop expanded along the Arcade and into Old Christchurch Road. The second of the shops to be occupied opened as a booksellers but he was also a photographer and publisher. In 1886 he produced *Bright's Guide to Bournemouth* and later Bright's map of Bournemouth and Neighbourhood.

By 1896 the new store on the site had the entrances paved with black and white mosaic featuring the name Bright's. Frederick Bright attended Richmond Hill Congregational Church^ where for 25 years he was secretary. The Bright's print works manager later became a partner and eventually succeeded the family as owner in 1924. Percy, who visited his birthplace in India, was a founder of the Bournemouth Natural Science Society and Mayor in 1929-30. The shop, now a House of Fraser store, changed its name to Dingles in 1974.

BRITTAIN, Vera (1893-1970), author and mother of Shirley Williams, lived in the New Forest. Just after the Second World War broke out Vera Brittain took her children into Bournemouth to buy clothes for the new term. There they found people carrying gas masks but otherwise she thought the town looked prosperous. The following year she attended the Labour Party Conference which met at Whitsun at the Pavilion and endorsed the war coalition.

The 1940 Whit weekend was in May and she stood outside the Highcliff Hotel marvelling at the hot sun, the scent of the pines and the yellow gorse on the cliff whilst thinking of those fighting abroad against the Germans in Belgium and Norway. Below to the east was the pier which would soon be partly destroyed as an anti-invasion precaution. Inside the hotel she watched members of Labour's National Executive waiting for the call from the new premier Winston Churchill* to join the war government. Later in her book *England's Hour* she looked back to the weekend and recalled "the incongruous luxuries of Bournemouth".

She was back in the town on 4 July 1942 to address a Peace Pledge Union meeting. Towards the end of the war daughter Shirley attended Talbot Heath School as a day girl whilst cycling daily from lodgings in Palmerston Road.

BROAD, Mary Aylett (1860-1942), founder of Talbot Heath School, travelled to Bournemouth in 1885 to find a school for sale. She bought Cranleigh Ladies School 6 Bradburne Road near the Triangle and the following year reopened it with thirty girls. Her model was North London Collegiate School although she ran a more liberal regime. In 1888 the school moved to Court Hill in Norwich Avenue where it eventually took over eight houses including Ardnaree and Woodborough (now Norwich Mansions). A decade later, having left the Baptist Church to join the Church of England, she handed the school to the Winchester Diocese which renamed it Bournemouth High School^ but she remained headmistress until 1924. Her pupils included Rosamund Essex*, Dilys Powell*, Fanny Cradock* and Lucy Faithful*.

She eventually moved to Surrey but returned in 1933 to lay the foundation stone of the new building above Pug's Hole in Talbot Woods. She was also present in 1935 when the Archbishop of York William Temple opened the completed complex and the school was renamed Talbot Heath.

BROOKE, Rupert (1887-1915), poet, regularly stayed with his two aunts at Grantchester Dene in Littledown Road. (The house, marked by a plaque erected by former Mayoress Joan Willoughby in 1965, is now 48 Dean Park Road following the building of the Wessex Way.) It was at this curiously named house that nine year old Brooke discovered poetry whilst browsing among Aunt Fanny's many books. The house had been bought by his great uncle Richard England Brooke, former Rector of Bath. On Sundays Rupert accompanied the aunts, Richard's daughters, to Holy Trinity Church^ where the vicar was AS Blunt, father of Anthony Blunt*. Aunt Fanny was the parish's Church Missionary Society honorary secretary.

Brooke as usual spent the 1907 summer at Grantchester Dene and during the Christmas holiday he wrote a letter from Bournemouth in which he rejected the class war and suggested that the spirit of socialism seemed as important as the dogma.

In 1910 two weeks of the annual Fabian Society summer school were given over to the National Committee for the Prevention of Destitution. He was present with the poet James Elroy Flecker* and afterwards Brooke spent part of July alone touring the south in a horse-drawn caravan speaking in favour of Beatrice Webb's* Poor Law Commission Minority Report. But he passed through Bournemouth without a pause in case his Tory aunts should see him before stopping to speak to crowds in Poole High Street.

With the outbreak of the Great War, Brooke, who was in the Navy, received at Portsmouth a parcel of wool clothing sent on behalf of the Mayor and Corporation of Bournemouth. In December 1914 Brooke was back in Bournemouth where he saw a poster advertising a play at the Theatre Royal^ in Albert Road starring his friend Cathleen Nesbitt who in 1912 had supplanted Noel Olivier as his girlfriend. Before joining his unit at Blandford he had stopped at Canford where he wrote the first line of *The Soldier* ("If I should die, think only this of me."). In the New Year, after a last visit to Littledown Road, he sailed from England never to return. He wrote to Cathleen from a ship off Gallipoli just a month before his death.

BULWER-LYTTON, 1st Lord (Edward) (1803-1873), politician and novelist, lived at Fulham's original Craven Cottage and introduced the well-known phrases 'the pen is mightier than the sword' and 'the great unwashed' into the English language. He spent the winter of 1849 at Adelaide Villa whose driveway entrance is now Adelaide Lane at the side of Bath Travel in Albert Road where a gatepost survives. At the time he was having success with the publication of his book *The Caxtons*.

BURROWS, Hedley (1887-1983), Dean of Hereford, became vicar of St Peter's Church in January 1936 just before sacristan Harry Crumpler, who had been appointed by the first vicar Morden Bennett*, retired. During the Second World War Burrows introduced Christmas Midnight Mass. In 1942 he invited Robert Price* to be senior curate and priest-in-charge of St Swithun's Church. That year St Peter's Church just missed being demolished in a massive bombing raid. Burrows lead a team forming a chain to lift buckets from a tap below to tower to counter the sparks from the demolished Beales. Two months later he was asked by the Bishop to be Archdeacon of Winchester. His son Simon, who was eight when the family arrived at St Peter's Church, became Bishop of Buckingham.

BURTON, Decimus (1800-1881), architect whose work includes Hyde Park Corner Screen and Wellington Arch. He succeeded Benjamin Ferrey* in 1847 as architect to Sir George Tapps-Gervis*. Unlike his predecessor, Burton did not know the area. He first visited in 1840 when invited by the owner of a property on Richmond Hill. In 1845 Burton wrote in a report: "The wooded valley through which the Bourne rivulet flows to the sea is and must always constitute the principal object in the landscape, and therefore any work undertaken there should be most jealously watched, and every endeavour made to preserve the natural beauty of the valley." It is due to him that there is a wide strip of open ground along the top of the East Cliff.

In 1848 he laid out the paths and shrubbery on the west side of Westover Road. His recommendation that the adjoining valley should be transformed into gardens was eventually made a reality in 1873. However his 1848 report led to the building of the first proper bridge across the River Bourne in The Square – although this name was not used until 1858. For many years coaches and riders had forded the stream whilst pedestrians had used a plank. Burton's connection with the Meyrick estate lasted until 1870.

C

CAIRNS, Lord (1819-1885), Lord Chancellor. In 1873 he built gothic-style Lindisfarne (now Earl's Court), his home in Gervis Road, where rooms were available for holidays to staff of the Bible-Women Nurses Association and the London City Mission. Personal visitors included Sir Henry Reeve* who was so taken with the area that he became a resident. On Sundays Cairns attended Holy Trinity Church^ where his brother-in-law Canon Eliot* was vicar. In 1878 the Lord Chancellor laid the foundation stone of The Hahnemann House^ which he officially opened the following year. Cairns died at home and was buried in Bournemouth Cemetery^.

CALLAGHAN, James (1912-2005), Prime Minister. Shortly after succeeding Harold Wilson* as Prime Minister, he addressed the Post Office Workers' conference. On the same day he met Labour Party members at Lincoln Hall^ where he paid tribute to "an outpost of the Labour Party in a Tory area". The Union Jack flew over the Highcliff Hotel during his lunch there. Within a fortnight he was back to have lunch at the Marsham Court Hotel and address the GMWU union conference at The Pavilion. His headline-making speech rejected further public spending. In 1980, a year after defeat, he returned as Opposition Leader to address a union conference and declare that he was very much alive. This fighting speech followed reports that Tony Benn and Barbara Castle wanted him to stand down.

In May 1989, when he had relinquished the Labour Leadership and was writing his memoirs, he attended the funeral in St Peter's Church of his cousin Ivor Jeffrey-Machin*. Afterwards the former premier, with his wife Audrey and daughter Margaret (Lady Jay), supported Ivor's widow Brenda by receiving the mourners at a tea reception at the Royal Bath Hotel.

CARPENTER, Thelma (1911-1998), snooker and billiard champion. Her father owned the Solent Cliffs Hotel which had two billiard rooms used by great players. New Zealand champion Clark McConarchy coached her on the beach, helping with her technique. She never went to school. She won the Women's Amateur Billiards Championship in 1932. Later she commentated on billiards for the BBC. The hotel site is now occupied by the BIC^

(Bournemouth International Centre) where snooker championships are televised.

CARTWRIGHT, Sir Charles (1862-1959), former post-boy and Bournemouth's longest serving mayor, moved to the town in 1898 and worked at the South-Western Hotel (now Sound Circus). Later he owned the nearby Railway Hotel (see Tony Hancock*) and the Norfolk Hotel. He was elected to the council in 1910 and served as mayor from 1919 to 1923 and again for a year from November 1928. These were years of enormous progress. During his mayoralty the Mont Dore Hotel became the Town Hall. In 1925, whilst out of office, he was invited to lay the foundation stone of The Pavilion.

As mayor he welcomed the Duke of Gloucester when he opened the building. The same year the council chamber was added to the Mont Dore building. He was living at Saxon, 17 St Anthony's Road, when he first became Mayor but had moved to number 12 by the time he served his last term. He was knighted a decade later. His chaplains for both his periods of office were from the Sacred Heart Church opposite the Norfolk Hotel. His friends included Sir Henry Page-Croft*.

CARTWRIGHT, Dame Mary (Lucy) (1900-1908), mathematician and Mistress of Girton. She was sent by her father, rector of Aynho in Northamptonshire, to board at Grovely Manor School (now Shelley Park^) in 1915 for two years. Afterwards she went to the Godolphin School in Salisbury until the end of the First World War. She lost one brother Nigel just before starting at the Boscombe school and another just after starting at Salisbury. They are both commemorated at Langton Matravers where they had attended Durnford School.

CASSEL, Sir Ernest (1852-1921), banker, lived at Branksome Dene (now Zetland Court) in Alumhurst Road from 1903. Winston Churchill*, who had known the house when it was the seaside home of his aunt Lady Wimborne*, was a guest in June 1918 when he was First Lord of Admiralty. His wife Clemmie had been there at the end of May with Alice Keppel. After Sir Ernest's death his sister Minna lived there. His granddaughter Lady Mountbatten* sold the estate in 1927.

CASTLE, Barbara (1910-2002), cabinet minister, visited Bournemouth in 1967 to inaugurate the electric train service. Afterwards she visited Labour Hall^.

Boscombe Manor (Grovely Manor School)
Dame Mary Cartwright boarded here.
Elizabeth Clarke was also educated here

Southbourne Pier, part of Southbourne developed by Dr Thomas Compton

CHARLES II (1630-1685) is thought to have spent a night at Muccleshell Hall (now a farmhouse) in Bury Lane at Throop during his secret 45-day journey across southern England in 1651 following his defeat by Oliver Cromwell at the Battle of Worcester. The King sailed to France from Shoreham. The house dates from about 1587 and was thatched until 1729.

CHRISTY, Edmund (1827-1902), St Clement's Church benefactor, came to the town from Aberdeen and from 1864 to 1866 was churchwarden of St Peter's Church. He suggested to the vicar Morden Bennett* that he would finance a new church near his new house if it could have its own parish carved out of the huge St Peter's parish. In 1871 Bennett laid the foundation stone of the church. The completed Bath stone building, which cost £30,000 and had a double nave, was consecrated by the Bishop of Winchester in 1873. 'Soapy Sam', as the evangelical Bishop Samuel Wilberforce was known, insisted that the candles were extinguished and the communion wafers replaced with bread. However, Christy's church was, from the beginning, a leading example of the Anglo-catholic tradition. His nearby Tudor style brick house, The Knole^, was completed the same year with its own chapel. JD Sedding, a pupil of George Street*, was architect of both. Christy moved to London soon after the church opened. The Knole was later the home of Sir Henry Page-Croft* and is now a Masonic lodge. The carriage entrance in Knyveton Road has become Knole Gardens.

Edmund Christy's brother JL Christy presented the church's stone reredos which was the largest since the Reformation. It is also the work Sedding, churchwarden at St Alban's Holborn, who included the figure of St Alban.

CHURCHILL, Sir Winston (1874-1965), statesman. While staying in 1893 with his aunt Lady Wimborne* at her seaside house Branksome Dene (now Zetland Court) in Alumhurst Road, the 18 year old was playing on a bridge spanning a corner of Branksome Dene Chine when he found himself cornered by both his brother and cousin and decided to slide down a pine tree. However, he fell 29 feet and his companions rushed back to the house to report that he had, "jumped over the bridge and won't speak to us". He remained unconscious for three days and doctors called from London discovered a ruptured kidney and a broken shoulder. During his convalescence Winston met leading statesmen and spent time in the House of Commons gallery. As a result he resolved to enter Parliament.

He stayed at the house in "salubrious Bournemouth" in June 1916 having just resigned his army commission and awaiting the fall of Asquith and again in 1918.

In 1935 he travelled first class by train to Bournemouth intending to speak on rearmament at the Conservative Party Conference but it was another Conference which was to make him Prime Minister. In May 1940 a meeting of the Labour Party National Executive Committee in the basement of the Highcliff Hotel led to the sudden resignation of Chamberlain as Prime Minister and Churchill becoming leader of the wartime coalition.

The following July he inspected coastal defences at Branksome Dene Chine and, gazing out to sea, recalled to General Sir Alan Brooke that he had spent some of his childhood there.

CLARK, Cumberland (1862-1941), playwright, poet and prolific author. The former sheep farmer, gold miner and church minister arrived in Bournemouth following the death of his wife. At first he lived in the Palace Court Hotel^. He wrote 68 books including the *Bournemouth Song Book* featuring local places and shops. As author of several books on Shakespeare, he became President of the Bournemouth Shakespeare Society. He worshipped at the Congregational Church^ in Richmond Hill and was killed when a bomb hit his nearby flat in Fern Bank, St Stephen's Road in April 1941. He had already designed his own tomb for Boscombe Cemetery.

CLARK, Ethel (1896-1976), police officer's widow who helped to catch two of the Great Train Robbers. In August 1963 she called the police when two men paid three months rent in used ten shilling notes for her garage at 45 Tweedale Road. The Buckinghamshire robbery had taken place just a week earlier and was still making headlines. Mrs Clark had advertised her garage in a shop window and felt suspicious about William Boal and Roger Cordrey (the only one of the fifteen-strong gang to plead guilty later). Whilst detectives were at her house, the men turned up in a van and a struggle followed before arrests were made. £140,000 was found in the vehicle and a further £5,910 in their rented flat above Mould's florist at 935 Wimborne Road. She received reward money and also threats which led to her selling the house and leaving town. But before moving she welcomed the train driver Jack Mills, who had been injured during the robbery, and his wife for a holiday.

CLARK, Sir James (1788-1870), doctor whose patients included John Keats for his last four months in Rome and Queen Victoria for the first 25 years of her reign. He lived at Eagles Nest, the former home of Lord Herbert* (BIC^ Purbeck Hall site). Clark believed that the pines contributed to a healthy environment and was probably responsible for Benjamin Disraeli* spending a long convalescence in the town. In 1863 he was visited by Princess Louise*,

Queen Victoria's daughter.

CLARKE, Elizabeth (1915-1993), Headmistress of Benenden School who raised academic standards, welcomed Princess Anne as a pupil and was appointed a CVO by the Queen. Elizabeth was born in Dorset and educated at Grovely Manor School^.

CLEAL, Edward (1858-1954), congregational minister and author, was appointed in 1890 by Richmond Hill Congregational Church^ for the Winton mission and opened Winton Congregational Church on Peter's Hill (Iceland site) in 1895. He founded a Penny Bank, a Band of Hope to counter the beer retailer next door on the corner of Luther Road, a cricket club and a library. In 1892 he formed the Bournemouth Fabian Society branch with fellow Congregationalist George Underwood (see Florence Underwood*).

COBHAM, Sir Alan (1894-1973), aviation pioneer knighted in 1926 after flying from Australia to land on the River Thames in front of the Houses of Parliament. In 1934 he founded a company to develop air to air refuelling. Four years earlier he had identified East Parley as a site "capable of being made into a magnificent aerodrome" which became Hurn Airport and is now Bournemouth International Airport. In 1935, after the success of 'Cobham's Flying Circus' displays, he started Cobham Air Routes which used Hurn as well Guernsey, Croydon and Portsmouth airfields. After the Second World War he lived at Falaise, a house built in 1913 in West Overcliff Drive, where he hosted a Bournemouth Symphony Orchestra fête attended by Sir Charles Groves*. Sir Alan Cobham was chairman of the Western Orchestral Society and during a financial crisis he donated a car for a raffle to save the orchestra. After the death of his wife actress Gladys Marie Lloyd in 1961 he devoted himself to establishing a new factory near Wimborne. In 1969 he handed over the chairmanship of Flight Refuelling, now Cobham plc, to his son Michael and the following year sold Falaise. Sir Alan died whilst visiting his son Geoffrey in Bournemouth.

COMPTON, Dr Thomas (1838-1925), founder of Southbourne, first knew the area as a student when he arrived in Christchurch to sail to Studland. In 1866 he moved to Holmwood 18 Christchurch Road (since demolished) and ran a surgery in Old Christchurch Road. In 1870 he bought a mile of open seafront land east of a track (Clifton Road) and called the quarter of a mile wide strip first 'South Bourne' and later 'Southbourne-on-Sea'. This high table of land, being one of the sunniest places in the country and having not only sea breezes but also winds from the Avon Valley to the north, was considered more bracing than Bournemouth. The following year he formed a company which built Belle Vue Road and in 1874 erected (on the west side of the present Bolton Road) a large glasshouse called a Winter Garden.

In 1875, the year he bought Cellars Farm on the eastern boundary, he moved to Southbourne where at first his home was the isolated house Clarenzia. After a year he moved to Locksley (now St Peter's School) where his family had five servants, a coachman and a groom. In 1881 Dr Compton built the South Cliff Hotel (since demolished) at the Crossroads and the following year formed the Southbourne on Sea Freehold Land Company Limited. A promenade was completed in 1885 and a terrace of six houses added, with Dr Compton living a number 4. A pier long enough to be served by steamers followed in 1888. However, bad weather at the turn of the century severely damaged the promenade and pier. With no money for essential repairs, the scheme including the seafront houses was abandoned.

At a London auction in 1901 the properties and vacant building plots failed to reach the reserve price and were sold privately at considerable loss. The Winter Garden had already been dismantled due to competition from Bournemouth's own Winter Gardens^. Dr Compton left Southbourne for Devon in 1892 when prospects for development still looked promising. He eventually returned in 1920 to live at Sandymount in Southbourne.

CONNAUGHT, 1st Duke of (1850-1942), Queen Victoria's son and Governor General of Canada, visited Bournemouth in 1892 to open a new wing of Boscombe Hospital. The following year he opened the Grand Continental Arcade (Boscombe Arcade). On both occasions he was entertained at the Royal Exeter Hotel.

COOPER DEAN, James Edward (1840-1921), landowner, who to his surprise in 1887 inherited Littledown House (now JP Morgan) and much surrounding and nearby land, including Dean Park and the West Cliff, from his childless cousin William Clapcott Dean*. The house was built in the 1780s and had a view of Christchurch Priory Church.

In 1896 James Cooper Dean gave the land for St Ambrose Church and in 1901 he gave, at a nominal rent, land to enable the council to lay out the West Overcliff Drive and Argyle Gardens.

In 1898 he had bought Iford Farm to prevent development spoiling his view from Littledown House. In 1904 he bought Stoke Wood House at Droxford in Hampshire for his two daughters. In 1913 Stoke Wood Road was laid out on his Northwood Estate which embraced the Wimborne Road cemetery. The first houses were at the south end whilst Iddesleigh and Grafton Roads continued to be given over to market gardening. Iddesleigh Road houses were built after the First World War.

In 1905 he was thrown from his carriage at Iford Bridge when the horses were frightened by cyclists and walked back to Littledown.

Just as William had given the town its cricket ground so in 1910 the family gave land, Dean Court, for the football club then called Boscombe Football Club.

COX, Freddie (1920-1973), Arsenal football player, was Bournemouth & Boscombe Football Club manager from 1956 to 1958 and returned for five years in 1965. During the 1956-7 season he saw the team make a surprise bid for the FA Cup by defeating Wolves and Spurs before being defeated by Manchester United on home ground. There was enormous excitement in the town with shops having special window displays and Malmesbury & Parsons' milk bottle tops decorated with cherries. Whilst still manager he ran a newsagents at 21 Charminster Road near his home at 58 Richmond Park Avenue.

CRABBE CREEKE, Christopher (1820-1886), architect and Architecture Association founder member, moved to Bournemouth in 1852 having been struck by its beauty. His first commission was to enlarge Boscombe Manor^ for Sir Percy Shelley*. The town commissioners appointed him as the first Surveyor and Inspector of Nuisances. He laid out the Wimborne Road cemetery and designed its chapel. As in his later design for the Dean Park estate, there are no straight lines. He resigned as Surveyor in 1879 and was elected a commissioner in 1883. He also worked for the Branksome Towers estate and Cooper Dean estate. His buildings include Talbot Village almshouses, Lansdowne Baptist Church and Hahnemann House^. In 1870 he designed Daniel Defoe's new tombstone for London's Bunhill Fields. Crabbe Creeke lived at Lainston Villa (since demolished) at the junction of Exeter Lane and Exeter Road in The Square and is buried in his cemetery.

CRADOCK, Fanny (1909-1993), early newspaper restaurant critic and pioneer television cook. Her rich father was constantly on the move; from the age of 15, as Phyllis Pechey, she attended Bournemouth High School^.

CREIGHTON, Connie (1935-2009), entertainer who toured with the Sooty Show as co-presenter with Harry Corbett and later his son Matthew Corbett until 1998. She was born at 139 Kinson Road and studied at the Bournemouth

College of Art. She had appeared with Sooty in the town and as late as 2007 addressed The Royal British Legion Women's Section conference at the BIC^. Although in later life she spent more time in Southport, where she was well-known and where she met her husband John Seaton in 1987, she returned to the house where she had been born for her final illness. John nursed her until her death in the family house. Her funeral was at nearby St Mark's Church in Talbot Village.

CROFT-COOKE, Rupert (1903-1979), obsessive autobiographer, moved to Bournemouth in 1973 following ill health. His record breaking 24 volume autobiography, which he completed at his flat in Amira Court in Bourne Avenue, recorded his life as a biographer, novelist, journalist, playwright, lecturer and intelligence officer as well as his friendships with such figures as Lord Alfred Douglas. Rupert died at home two years after *The Green Green Grass*, the final volume of his autobiography, had been published.

CROMER, 1st Lord (1841-1917), diplomat, declined a Westminster Abbey grave to be buried with his first wife in Bournemouth Cemetery^. Lady Cromer had died in Cairo in 1898 where her husband was engaged in vital diplomacy administering the Anglo-Egyptian agreement which he had devised.

Bournemouth was chosen for her burial as she had happy memories of visiting the town with her children. Lord Cromer was unable to be present but both sons attended the funeral at the Sacred Heart Church. On the same day as Lord Cromer's burial there were memorial services at Westminster Abbey and in Cairo.

CUTLER, Joseph (1830-1910), builder and early supporter of women's suffrage, was born into a Christchurch fishing family. He moved to Bournemouth with his wife Emma who had refused to go back to Australia where they had lived for a time. He joined a building firm but after a few months started his own business and the following year built Durley Dean (now a hotel). Soon afterwards he built Muriel, later the home of Aubrey Beardsley*. Cutler's image appears on tiles at Joseph's Terrace 216-226 Old Christchurch Road built in the 1880s. In 1881 he was elected a commissioner^ and advocated that the town should petition for council status under the 1882 Municipal Corporations Act. When the authority was established he served as a councillor and alderman. In 1883 he salvaged timber from the storm-damaged Pier to build steps up the West Cliff by his bathing machines. The route, once known as Joseph's Steps, survives as the West Cliff Zigzag. He gave the monkey puzzle trees in Bournemouth Cemetery.

Christopher Crabbe Creeke

Joseph Cutler

D

DAINTON, Barbara West (1911-2007), the last but one survivor of the Titanic disaster, was born in Bournemouth in May 1911, just ten months before the ship's maiden voyage. The family was emigrating to Florida on board the Titanic. After her father Edwy waved to his wife Ada and two daughters in a lifeboat he was never seen again. They presumed he had drowned and with no home to return to in Bournemouth, the bereaved family came back to Britain and eventually lived in the parents' home county of Cornwall. Barbara never spoke outside the family about the tragedy.

DARBY, John Nelson (1800-1882), influential Plymouth Brethren member and leader of the breakaway Darbyites or, as known abroad, Darbistes. He travelled all over the world for forty years but after a fall at Dundee in 1881 he stayed with a friend Henry A Hammond at Sundridge House (Queen's Hotel site) on corner of Gervis and Meyrick Roads. Darby died there the following year and was buried in Bournemouth Cemetery. His grave began attracting visitors from Germany, where he was well known for his translation of the Bible.

DARWIN, Charles (1809-1882), naturalist. In 1862, three years after publishing *The Origin of Species*, Darwin arrived in Bournemouth on 1 September to stay at the thatched Cliff Cottage (BIC^ site). The rustic cottage, one of the town's first houses and the seaside house of the Drax family of Charborough Park in Dorset, was surrounded by a low wall of brown stones brought from Charborough. This survived along the west side of Exeter Road and into South Cliff Road until 1984 when the BIC was built over the cottage site and its former driveway Cliff Cottage Road.

Darwin brought his parents and son Leonard who was recovering from scarlet fever on the visit. His wife was found to have contracted the disease and a separate house was rented for her. Medicines were bought from Blacklock's^ chemist (now Miss Selfridge) in The Square whose owner Frank Spinney, pharmacist and botanist, helped Darwin search boggy Poors Common (now Meyrick Park where there was a tributary of the Bourne) for specimens of the sundew. During his first week Darwin wrote home to his Kent neighbour Lord

Avebury (the inventor of Bank Holidays): "I long to be at home and at steady work." Later he wrote to botanist and traveller Sir Joseph Hooker saying: "This is a nice, but most barren country, and I can find nothing to look at. Even the brooks and ponds produce nothing. The country is like Patagonia."

Although he found nothing to interest him in the River Bourne he did manage to work on his book *Insectivorous Plants* which was eventually published in 1875. He also walked on nearby heath land studying heather flowers perforated by bees from hives and included this research in his 1871 book *Cross and Self-fertilization of Plants*. He was due home at Downe in Kent on 30 September but managed to leave four days early. In the end he did so much work during his month at Cliff Cottage that he was too tired to undertake a planned visit to the British Association in London.

During Easter 1882 daughter Henrietta Litchfield stayed in Bournemouth to enable her father's house at Downe to be quiet during his dying days.

DAVIES, John Trevor (1907-1974), Congregational minister. Dr Davies became Minister of Richmond Hill Congregational Church^ in 1951. During his twenty years ministry there he saw the congregation grow and his abilities were recognised in 1960 when he became chairman for a year of the Congregational Union of England and Wales. He was also known to a wider public through his late night epilogues for local regional ITV. He retired in 1971 following ill health.

DAY, Robert (1822-1873), Bournemouth's first photographer, was Norfolk-born and came to the town in 1862 from nearby Hampreston where he had been a 'farming bailiff'. He lived with his wife and children on the east side of Holdenhurst Road (Lloyds site) between Cotlands and St Swithun's Roads. His studio was next to St Andrew's Church (the 'Scotch Church' on the site of NatWest at the bottom of Richmond Hill) in Old Christchurch Road. He offered views of the area, on his *cartes de visite*, to visitors. Residents were tempted by the opportunity to have their house, horses or family graves photographed. He was pleased to have a reputation for a sharp print and followed the latest development of the invention. "Ladies and children's portraits" were taken by his daughter Harriet "if preferred".

Day was a corporal in the 19th Hants Volunteers. After suffering poor health he died in 1873 and was given a military funeral St Peter's Church conducted by Philip Eliot*, vicar of the new Church of the Holy Trinity.

The business continued in the hands of Robert's wife Emily and son William as Day & Son. By now the family was living in a cottage in Lansdowne Road. His sister Mary also helped and not only always encouraged her brother but became a noted photographer herself. Leslie Ward* was a great friend of William and taught his niece Margaret at Bournemouth School of Art.

Many of Robert and William's photographs are in the Bournemouth Library.

DEAN, William Clapcott (1812-1887), banker and landowner who lived at Littledown (now JP Morgan), was a co-founder of the Christchurch, Wimborne and Ringwood Bank with George Adams and railway pioneer William Castleman. In 1856 he became one of the first commissioners^. He gave a 999 year lease at a nominal rent to Hahnemann House^. His pack of harriers was taken as far as central Bournemouth. He was succeeded at Littledown by James Cooper Dean*.

DE VASCONCELLOS, Josefina (1904-2005), sculptor who at the age of 90 made the Statue of Reconciliation for Coventry Cathedral. She was the daughter of a Brazilian diplomat and an English doctor who during the First World War sent her for her first drawing lessons to the Bournemouth School of Art^ at The Lansdowne.

DIANA, Princess of Wales (1961-1997), first wife of Prince Charles, flew by helicopter to Meyrick Park in 1987 to open the McCarthy & Stone headquarters in Oxford Road. In 1991 she landed by helicopter at Wentworth College to visit the nearby Anglo-European College of Chiropractic where she was patron.

DISRAELI, Benjamin (1804-1881), Prime Minister. Having just stepped down as Chancellor of the Exchequer he visited the 3rd Lord Malmesbury at Hurn Court on Boxing Day 1853. Suffering from gout in the first year of his second term as premier, Disraeli was advised by Queen Victoria to "try the very salubrious air of Bournemouth" where her doctor James Clark* had lived. Disraeli arrived at the Royal Bath Hotel in November 1874. At first he thought the town to be "an overgrown watering place", the food to be "frightful" and the climate "savage". He wrote: "I detest the place, it is a large overgrown watering-place, almost as bad as Torquay." He went for a walk in the snow.

By 10 December he was able to write to The Queen: "The visit to this place, which Your Majesty deigned to recommend, will turn out a great success.

"The weather has been too variable; one day it was like the Cornishe, so soft and sunny, the Isle of Wight looming, and yet not distant, and the waters glittering in the bay-like coast. But storm has prevailed, and nothing but the bending pines could have withstood its violence." He added that he was enjoying reading the *Life of the Prince Consort.*

However, on Christmas Eve he wrote to Lady Bradford: "The severe weather has been very trying to me." By 3 January he wrote to Lady Chesterfield: "The thaw has quite revived me and removed all my malaise." Work in Bournemouth included preparing a New Year Honours' List for The Queen. Recommendations included the Grand Cross of the Order of the Bath for essayist Thomas Carlyle and a baronetcy for Tennyson but both declined.

The Chancellor of the Exchequer Sir Stafford Northcote dined with Disraeli on his birthday 21 December. The Prime Minister returned to London in January.

DOBELL, Horace (1828-1917), brother of poet Sydney Dobell and founder of Mont Dore 'residential and bath establishment', moved to Bournemouth in 1882 to open a building for the treatment of people with 'Affections of the Throat, Chest and Mucous Membranes' as well as 'Rheumatic, Gouty, Syphilitic and other Morbid Constitutional States'. The foundation stone had been laid the year before by King Oscar* of Sweden. It was called Mont Dore after the Mont Dore Cure then available at Mont-Dore-les-Bains, in Auverigne, France. Its principal physician was installed at Dobell's Mont Dore as Resident Medical Officer and water was brought from the Auverigne thermal springs.

This new Mont Dore designed for 120 resident patients had a luxurious Turkish Bath, halls for inhalation of vapours, a reading room, a general dining room and a smoking room. Dr Dobell, a prolific author, published *The Medical Aspects of Bournemouth* in which he praised the chines as "arteries through which the pure sea air penetrates to the crowded thoroughfares of the town" and "the resinous emanations from the pines".

Mont Dore was extended in 1888 and in 1892 Dobell retired to a specially built house in Parkstone with views of the Isle of Purbeck. Mont Dore was requisitioned during the First World War first as a hospital for Indian soldiers and then an officers' convalescent home. In 1921 it became the Town Hall with the carriage entrance converted into front entrance.

DRIBERG, Tom (1905-1976), journalist, politician and communist. In 1924, shortly after he had been expelled from Lancing College he took a job at a Bournemouth prep school. His duties included taking the boys to the beach for swimming which he found to be an alarming responsibility. He described St Stephen's Church as "prosperous and smug". During the Second World War he was recruited as a spy but was later exposed by Anthony Blunt*.

DRIVER, William (1759-1819), nurseryman, Surveyor to the Crown Estate and son of Samuel who founded surveyors Drivers Jonas. William and his Poole-born wife Ann, along with their three daughters, lived in a detached house in Surrey Square, off London's Old Kent Road, which had been developed by his mother Jane who inherited the land from her uncle.

In 1786-7 William and his brother Abraham, along with Thomas Richardson and William King, helped to compile the first detailed map of the New Forest for a Royal Commission report. The Drivers Map was the basis sixty years later for the New Forest's first Ordnance Survey six inch map.

In 1802 William bid at an auction held at The George Inn in Christchurch for some "Waste Grounds" in Bournemouth being offered by the Enclosure Commissioners^ administering the 1802 Christchurch Enclosure Act. The following year he bought more "allotments" in the area. His holdings were alongside the east side of the Bourne Stream north of the Square to near the county boundary, a strip running north-east from there over the future East Avenue to the bend in Wimborne Road (south of Winton) and at Moordown around the current Cowper Road area. The latter was sold by him as early as 1807 and later he disposed of the rest.

His marriage to the daughter of Samuel White of Poole resulted in William being invited by the Mayor of Poole to be one of three commissioners^ appointed to administer the 1805 Great Canford Enclosure Act.

DRUITT, James (1845-1929), first Town Clerk, succeeded his father as clerk to the commissioners^ in 1877. When in 1890 the town was granted its charter, which he received and read aloud, he became Town Clerk. During the next twelve years he oversaw the extension of the borough boundaries and purchase of land. In 1914, just after the outbreak of the First World War, he was installed as Mayor. The ceremony was the last to take place in the old Winter Gardens^ where he had once been the company's solicitor. He lived first in Avenue Road (Superdrug site) when in 1871 he went into partnership with his cousin and fellow solicitor W Harvey Druitt. In 1874 he married Augusta and the following year moved to Avebury in Madeira Road (southeast corner of Trinity Road). He was active in the town and a churchwarden of St Peter's. His brother John was town clerk of Christchurch and another brother Herbert was an historian whose collection formed the basis for the Red House Museum. A cousin Montague Druitt was wrongly named as the notorious Jack the Ripper murderer.

DRUMMOND, Sir John (1934-2006), writer, broadcaster and BBC Promenade Concert Director, was on holiday in Bournemouth when war was declared in 1939 and the family stayed. His mother rented a house at Iford

Sir Henry Drummond Wolff

Mont Dore Hotel (now Bournemouth Town Hall)
Built by Horace Dobell

whilst working at Shelley Park^ issuing gas masks. Later she was employed in the canteen at The Metropole Hotel (Royal London House site) at The Lansdowne where Canadian troops were billeted.

With his father away at sea, Drummond fell more under the influence of his Australian mother, a singer, who had a passion for painting and poetry. She encouraged his piano lessons with her accompanist. Meanwhile he enjoyed spending much time in the Music Library at the Lansdowne and attended Bournemouth Municipal Orchestra concerts. A recital by Kathleen Ferrier led him twenty years later to make a film about the singer.

He was a pupil at Gorse Cliff School (since demolished) in Boscombe Spa Road for five years from 1943. He cycled daily from home and found both the headmaster Brian Mabley and the English teacher Frank Pickering inspirational as they opened up art, history, literature and correct English. He loved the beauty of St Stephen's Church and briefly considered pursuing a career in architecture. On Saturdays he often attended Bournemouth Film Society evenings at the Municipal College Hall. In 1948 he won a scholarship to Canford School and the family moved to Christchurch.

DRUMMOND WOLFF, Sir Henry (1830-1908), diplomat, Christchurch MP and Primrose League founder, lived at Boscombe Tower (Burlington site) in Owls Road from 1868. He laid out Boscombe Spa, including in 1874 the Boscombe Spa Hotel (now the Chine Hotel), and promoted the spring at the south entrance to Boscombe Gardens.

Thanks to the influence of Lord Malmesbury (3rd Earl)*, he was elected to Parliament where he introduced the House Occupiers' Disqualification Bill to allow a householder to let his house furnished for four months a year without losing a voting qualification. Sir William Harcourt called it "the Bournemouth Reform Bill".

In 1876 Sir Drummond Wolff performed the opening ceremony of the original Winter Gardens^ in Bournemouth. In 1888 he became chairman of the Boscombe Pier Company and invited Lady Shelley* to preside at the driving of the first pile amid great celebrations which included a lunch at the Chine Hotel. He was associated with *The Owl* magazine which is recalled by Owls Road. His appointment to the Eastern Roumelia Commission resulted in Roumelia Lane. The bridge in Boscombe Gardens replaces a rustic crossing erected by him.

DURRELL, Gerald (1925-1995), naturalist and zoologist, was educated at Wychwood School^. *My Family and Other Animals*, described by David Bellamy as "one of the best and most hilarious books you will read", was written by

Durrell in six weeks at the St Albans Avenue house of his sister Margo Durrell* where he kept animals. In 1950 six monkeys escaped and were found in garage in Chigwell Road, a shed in Howard Road and up a tree in Brackendale Road. In 1957 there were at least 400 animals including snakes and eagles in a tent and the garage. He also had a temporary menagerie in JJ Allen store opposite Beales. Having failed to find a site in Bournemouth for a zoo, despite the support of MP Nigel Nicolson*, Durrell founded the famous Les Augrès Manor zoological park in Jersey which, with the support of Princess Anne, teaches the practice of captive breeding and release back into the wild.

DURRELL, Lawrence (1912-1990). Poet, playwright, novelist and brother of Gerald Durrell* and Margo Durrell*. See Alan G Thomas*.

DURRELL, Margo (1919-2007), Gerald Durrell's sister, married pilot Jack Breeze, whom she had met in Corfu, at St Andrew's Church in Bennett Road before living in South Africa. Later she ran a boarding house at 51 St Albans Avenue in Bournemouth where her brother Gerald Durrell* kept animals collected on his trips abroad. She featured in Gerald's popular book *My Family and Other Animals* which was turned into a television series. She wrote her own story *Whatever Happened to Margo*, published in 1995, not just as the result the television adaptation, which she enjoyed, but largely because her granddaughter was impressed when finding in the attic Margo's early manuscript about her days as a landlady.

Edward VII arriving at the Royal Victoria Hospital (renamed Westbourne Hospital)

Bournemouth West Station (now demolished)
Edward VIII travelled from this station

E

EDEN, Sir Anthony (1897-1977), Prime Minister, stayed at The Carlton Hotel as premier whilst attending the 1955 Conservative Party Conference held at The Pavilion. His stay at the hotel was preceded by huge preparations. An entire suite was gutted, redecorated and refurnished for the Prime Minister's four day stay. When at two days' notice a further room for late night meetings was requested, in order not to disturb Sir Anthony's wife Clarissa, an adjoining bedroom was redecorated at speed. Other cabinet ministers staying at The Carlton included the Lord Chancellor Lord Kilmuir and Chancellor of the Exchequer Rab Butler. Foreign Secretary Harold Macmillan* was woken at 3.30 a.m. to receive a red box. He completed the enclosed work and handed the box back to the courier at 5 a.m. For the dining room a chef covered hams with white glaze to create portraits of Sir Anthony and Sir Winston Churchill*.

EDWARD VII (1841-1910), Prince Edward, when aged 15, and his tutor stayed incognito for a night in September 1856 at the (Royal) Bath Hotel. In the morning they wandered around the town before walking along the beach to Poole Harbour and spending a night at The Antelope in Poole High Street.

In 1877 he is understood to have helped Lillie Langtry* to build the Red House (now the Langtry Manor Hotel) in Derby Road where she occasionally entertained him.

In 1890, when as Prince of Wales he opened Westbourne Hospital^, he set out in a carriage from Canford accompanied by his son Prince George (the future George V*), his host Lady Wimborne and Lord Randolph Churchill (her brother and father of Winston). The Princess of Wales was unable to be present due to having caught flu. In the town the roads were decorated with fourteen evergreen arches. In The Square it took the form of the new Eiffel Tower. Two thousand flags had been borrowed from the Admiralty.

The Prince officially entered Bournemouth at Cemetery Junction and from there the route was down Lansdowne Road, St Paul's Road, Holdenhurst Road and Bath Hill. At the bottom a halt was made at the Royal Bath Hotel which had been lavishly decorated by owner Sir Merton Russell-Côtes* in honour of the Prince's second visit. As the four carriages arrived the Grenadier Guards band struck up the national anthem. The procession continued to the Pier

Approach and into the gardens for speeches in a pavilion. Afterwards the procession passed through The Square to Poole Road. Following the opening the Prince had lunch at Lady Wimborne's seaside house Branksome Dene^.

Afterwards the Prince visited St Peter's Church and the YMCA. The return journey to Canford, by way of Winton where people lined Wimborne Road, took an hour. Schoolchildren were presented with commemorative mugs bearing portraits of the Prince and the absent Princess.

EDWARD VIII (1894-1972), later the Duke of Windsor, visited Bournemouth as Prince of Wales in October 1927 to open the Boscombe Undercliff extension and the Prince of Wales Ward at Boscombe Hospital. During a packed day he attended a Scout, Guide and Boys Brigade rally at Meyrick Park, where *God Bless the Prince of Wales* was sung, and also visited the Town Hall, Winton, St Augustin's Church and Poole. Lunch was at the Royal Bath Hotel and tea at the Branksome Towers Hotel before he caught the 5 p.m. train at Bournemouth West Station (Queen's Road).

EGLINTON, John (1868-1961), author mentioned by James Joyce in *Ulysses*. In 1928, after working for 27 years (under his real name William Kirkpatrick Magee) at the National Library of Ireland, he retired on an early pension to Springhill, 21 Carbery Avenue where he wrote *Irish Literary Portraits* and *A Memoir of AE: George William Russell* who died at Stagsden Nursing Home (since demolished) at 16 West Cliff Road and edited the *Letters of George Moore.*

EISENHOWER, Dwight (1890-1969), US President, as a General in the Second World War, met Field-Marshall Montgomery* at The Carlton Hotel in 1944 to view the D-Day rehearsal in Poole Bay.

ELIOT, Philip (1835-1917), Dean of Windsor, was appointed the first Vicar of Holy Trinity Church^ in 1867 before the church was built during 1868 and 1869. The vicarage was built in 1873 and two years later one of the visitors was Beatrice Webb* whom he was preparing for confirmation. His brother-in-law was Lord Cairns* who attended the church. In 1884 Eliot, who was noted for his eloquent preaching, was made an honorary canon of Winchester Cathedral.

The following year he officiated at the funeral of Mary Anne Talbot* at Talbot Village as requested in her will and was rewarded with £300. The same year he was also involved in Lord Cairns' funeral service at Bournemouth Cemetery.

In 1883 Eliot married as his second wife Mary Pitt-Rivers, a member of the well-known Dorset family and descendant of William Pitt. She was also one of Queen Victoria's maids of honour. Eliot left Holy Trinity in 1891 at the Queen's invitation to became Dean of Windsor.

ELIZABETH, Empress (1837-1898), consort of Franz Josef I of Austria who was also known as Sisi. Her Majesty visited with her 20 year old daughter Archduchess Marie Valérie* and 28 staff for a week in 1888 staying at Newlyn's Family Hotel (now the Royal Exeter Hotel) which had been reserved "by Royal command" for ten days. Eight suites were booked with every windowsill filled with flowers supplied by a nursery in the Holdenhurst Road. The main corridor was fitted with seventy purple curtains tied back with ribbons in the gold and black Austrian colours.

The Empress had spent the Easter weekend in London confined to Claridge's with a sore throat. They arrived at Bournemouth East Station^ at 1.20 p.m. on a special six carriage train in record time from Waterloo on Easter Tuesday 10 April. The direct line from Christchurch had only recently opened. JJ Allen needed three removal vans to carry the luggage to the hotel. Proprietor Henry Newlyn, former Guards Club secretary, welcomed the Royal party with his daughters Florence and Leonie presenting bouquets. In the evening Prince Bernadotte* and his wife, just back from their honeymoon, and Baroness von Hügel* called. The following day the widow of Lord Cairns* called and the Swedish Lord Chamberlain arrived with an invitation to visit Queen Sofia* at Crag Head (since rebuilt as flats) in Manor Road.

The Royal doctor supervised the collection of milk from stables opposite, where a cow was kept. The Empress also liked to take sea water baths. Language difficulties were resolved by the gardener who wore a tabard with 'milk' written on the front and 'sea water' on the back. A slap on the back meant 'prepare a bath' whilst a poke in the chest indicated a request for milk.

The Empress walked everywhere and spent much time in the gardens and on the beach which she visited at 6 a.m. on her first morning. She even sat on a donkey. The Archduchess rode in an open carriage to explore Southbourne and Christchurch.

On Sunday the Archduchess attended the 8 a.m. Mass at the Sacred Heart Church whilst the Empress stayed indoors with a cold. Medicine was brought from Blacklock's^ chemist (now Miss Selfridge) in The Square.

The following day the Royal train arrived at the station at 8.50 a.m. which was just eight minutes before the Royal party was taking its leave of Mr and Mrs Newlyn at the hotel. An open carriage, watched by a crowd of about sixty, was waiting as the visitors' book was signed. The Empress found the hotel "so comfortable" and Bournemouth "one of the most charming places I have ever seen". The Swedish Lord Chamberlain was on the station platform to say farewell as the train pulled out for Newhaven where the Austrian party continued their journey to Baden Baden. This was less than a year before Elizabeth's son Rudolph was found shot dead at Mayerling and a decade before her assassination by an anarchist at Lake Geneva.

A legacy of the visit is the candle illuminations in the Lower Pleasure Gardens on Wednesdays in August. As it was the custom for Elizabeth's gardeners in Vienna to light the Schönbrunn Palace's garden paths with candles it was decided to provide similar illuminations in the grounds of the Winter Gardens^ which were put at her disposal. The Empress was so delighted that the idea was repeated in 1897 for Queen Victoria's Diamond Jubilee. The Empress allowed Henry Newlyn to fly her standard on Sundays and as a result Newlyn's Family Hotel was renamed Newlyn's Royal & Imperial Park Hotel.

ELIZABETH, Queen (1900-2002), the Queen Mother and consort of George VI*. In 1940, during the Second World War, the Queen paid a secret visit with the King to inspect troops. In May 1991, when she was 91 years old, Her Majesty landed by helicopter in Meyrick Park to visit the 70th anniversary conference of the Royal British Legion Women's Section at the BIC^. "I would like to express my deep appreciation for all your dedicated work," she told delegates who had presented her with purses from all over the country for the Widows and Ex-servicewomen's Allowance Scheme. Following tea, the Queen stood on the BIC steps to watch a march past of 300 standard bearers along Exeter Road.

EMBLETON, Ron (1930-1988), illustrator and cartoon strip artist. In 1962, shortly after being elected to the Royal Institute of Oil Painters, he moved to 50 Carbery Avenue where he continued his prolific output by turning Stingray and Captain Scarlet into a strip as well as working for *Girl's Crystal*, *June* and *Princess* annuals. In the 1970s he did paintings of the north-east, drawings for the Dickens series in *This England* and Wicked Wanda in *Penthouse*. His interest in the Roman period led him to produce paintings for the Museum of London.

EMPSON, John (1871-1952), Bournemouth's first Labour alderman and mayor, was an engraver for music publisher Novello and came to the town in 1899 due to ill health. He ran a succession of boarding houses in Southcote Road including number 46 called Newington after Newington Vestry in London where he was an elected member. The first Labour Party meetings were held at his house and he was elected Springbourne councillor in 1912. He was wartime Mayor in 1941-2 when, with Robert Old*, he was required to be willing to remain in town to negotiate should the Nazis invade.

Empress Elizabeth of Austria

Winter Gardens, showing candle illuminations

ENGLISH, Sir David (1931-1998), *Daily Mail* editor, attended Bournemouth School^ from 1941 to 1945 after his widowed mother and maternal grandparents moved to the town to run a hotel. These were war years and Taunton's School had been evacuated from Southampton to share the buildings and nearby church halls which were hired for the expanded school. Due to his auburn hair David was known to friends as William because he read all the *Just William* books in the public library. During these war years he overcame the shortage of comics by creating his own by hand and hiring the single copy out at a halfpenny a time. He once described his wartime childhood as like the film *Hope and Glory*. His mother wanted him to go to university but, maybe influenced by his Methodist grandfather who took three daily papers, David left school at 16 to study typing and shorthand and in 1946 joined *The Daily Echo* before moving to the *Christchurch Times* in 1948. It was his job to take the half made up pages by bus to the *Echo* on Richmond Hill and choose the large type for his headlines.

After a year he moved to Portsmouth on his way to becoming Editor of the *Daily Mail* (1971-1992) and group editor-in-chief. Lord Rothermere described him as "the greatest and most creative editor seen in Fleet Street since the time of Northcliffe" and *The Times* as "one of the most influential figures in British Journalism". Bournemouth University made him an honorary Doctor of Letters in 1995. He had a house at Brockenhurst enabling him to become a governor of his old school during his last four years. English was Associated Newspapers Chairman when six weeks before his death he was at the Wessex Hotel to present awards to *Echo* journalists.

One of the last pieces he wrote was for the Bournemouth Parry* Festival programme. He recalled his love for his school song *Jerusalem*. The school's Sir David English Sports Centre opened in 1999.

ESSEX, Rosamund (1900-1985), first woman editor of the *Church Times*. She joined the paper in 1929, worked with Edward Heath* and served as editor from 1950 to 1960, widening the readership. She still contributed in her retirement.

Her family came from Barnstable to live at 3 Borthwick Road when her father Herbert was appointed chaplain to Springbourne Orphanage (since closed) run by the Sisters of Bethany. During the First World War she was a day pupil at Bournemouth High School^ where she loved Greek and Latin and became a close friend of Dilys Powell*. Rosamund lost her brother in the war and remembered her form mistress saying: "I have come to tell you a very terrible fact. Only one out of ten of you girls can ever hope to marry. This is not a guess of mine. It is a statistical fact. Nearly all the men you might have married have been killed." Rosamund never married but she did take advantage of the new openings she was told were to be available to women.

She spent a lot of time at the nearby convent and on Sundays often attended the High Mass at St Clement's Church next door where it was difficult to find a free seat. The Anglo-Catholic vicar was the "the frightening Father CS Towle" (husband of Eleanor Taylor*). "Do you know the difference between a cope and a chasuble?" asked Rosamund years later when interviewing Monica Furlong for a job at the *Church Times*. Rosamund's father moved to the Isle of Dogs when she was 23.

EUGENIE, Empress (1826-1920), consort of Napoleon III. In 1881, when living in exile at Chislehurst, the widowed Empress visited Bournemouth. During her two hour visit to the Royal Bath Hotel she was amazed on entering a downstairs room to see a cabinet which had been in her boudoir at St Cloud. Sir Merton Russell-Côtes* had bought it in Glasgow from a man who had purchased items of art and furniture from a sale at the Palais Royale. The cabinet is now in the Russell-Côtes Art Gallery & Museum. The Empress called on Queen Sophia of Sweden* at her rented home Crag Head (since rebuilt as flats) in Manor Road.

EVANS, (Thomas) Eric (1928-1996), Dean of St Paul's Cathedral. He arrived in Bournemouth in 1958 to be a curate at St Peter's Church. Aware of a high number of suicides he was moved to found the Bournemouth Samaritans in 1961 at a meeting in St Peter's Hall, its first base. During the previous winter there had been Tuesday night training sessions with talks from Dr Doris Odlam*, Dr James Fisher and Samaritans founder Chad Varah. Evans left St Peter's Church in 1962; he claimed to have learnt how to organise a big service for national occasions whilst at St Peter's.

EXETER, Marchioness of (1757-1837), former Duchess of Hamilton and third wife of the 1st Marquess of Exeter who died in 1804. As a widow she lived from 1825 at Whithall Gardens in London and for a county home rented The Mansion (now the Royal Exeter Hotel) from Lewis Tregonwell*. Exeter Road is named after her.

The Bath Hotel (now Royal Bath Hotel) designed by Benjamin Ferrey

The East Cliff Hall (now Russell-Côtes Museum) designed by John Fogerty

F

FAITHFULL, Baroness (Lucy) (1910-1996), children's campaigner, attended Bournemouth High School^ and in 1977 was the guest at Talbot Heath School's speech day. Her father had been killed in the Great War when she was six. She died on the day sixteen children were murdered in Dunblane. Her memorial is The Lucy Faithfull Foundation which provides treatment and support for child abusers and their victims.

FERREY, Benjamin (1810-1880), architect of the Royal Bath Hotel and Bagshot Park (for the Duke of Connaught*; now home of Prince Edward). The son of Christchurch draper Benjamin Ferrey and younger brother of George Ferrey*, he attended Wimborne Grammar School and trained for seven years at Auguste Pugin's drawing school in London. A fellow pupil and friend was the teacher's son Augustus Pugin. In 1836 Ferrey was appointed estate architect by Sir George Tapps-Gervis (Meyrick)* who asked him to produce a development plan for the east side of the Bourne Chine including a line of different style houses for Westover Road. The plan for a Marine Village was shown at the Royal Academy of Arts Summer Exhibition although the proposed crescents of Italian and gothic villas were never built.

He also designed the (Royal) Bath Hotel which opened on Queen Victoria's Coronation Day in 1838. By 1840, when his father was Mayor of Christchurch, he was succeeded by Decimus Burton*. Ferrey's only surviving Bournemouth work is the core of the Royal Bath Hotel. Through Ferrey, Augustus Pugin soon came to know and love Christchurch Priory Church for which he designed an altar and where he arranged for his first wife to be buried.

FERREY, George (c1808-1893), organist at Christchurch Priory Church and older brother of Benjamin Ferrey*, was often at Boscombe Manor^ where he played pieces composed by Sir Percy Shelley*. Ferrey tuned pianos at many homes in Bournemouth.

FLECKER, James Elroy (1884-1915), poet, spent childhood holidays at Seacote (Greenways site) in Warren Edge Road in Southbourne. The house had been built by his father Dr WH Flecker, a clergyman and headmaster in

Cheltenham, following the birth of his sickly daughter Claire. She survived to write two books: *Starting Place of Prayer* (1929) and *The Road* (1935).

Flecker was christened Herman but called 'Roy' as a child and only adopted 'James' at Oxford. He loved roaming the cliffs and sand dunes near Hengistbury Head. Two years before the poet died he told a friend that his poem *Brumana*, written in Lebanon, was about how he found inspiration among the Bournemouth pines: "...dark militia of the southern shore / Old fragrant friends – preserve me the last lines / Of that long saga which you sang me, pines / When, lonely boy beneath the chosen tree/ I listened, with my eyes up on the sea."

FLEMING-WILLIAMS, Ian (1914-1998), painter, teacher and John Constable scholar. He was appointed art master at Canford School in 1937. During this time he began painting a six foot high mural on the stairs of Horace G Commin^, a large traditional bookshop at 100 Commercial Road. It featured Samuel Johnson and twenty of his contemporaries including James Boswell, Sir Joshua Reynolds, and Sir Horace Walpole. Research on each character and Fleming-Williams' five years in the Navy during the Second World War meant that progress was slow. In 1947 he moved to Charterhouse and had to travel back to Bournemouth to complete the work. After some years it was covered up by books but in 1978 shop owner John Ruston* had the work restored.

FOGERTY, John Frederick (1863-1942), architect. In 1886 the Irish architect began his practice in Shropshire but soon moved to an office in Belfast House in Gervis Place. He lived in Boscombe and then at 4 Talbot Road in Winton where he was responsible for the nearby Winton Hall cinema (Hop and Kilderkin site) which opened in 1908. He also designed St Peter's Hall. His most admired work is the Russell-Côtes Art Gallery and Museum which was built as East Cliff Hall^ to be home of Sir Merton and Lady Russell-Côtes*. The villa appears as Rudolph Valentino's Hollywood home in Ken Russell's 1977 film *Valentino*. The Fogerty family left the town in 1914.

FOREST, Antonia (1915-2003), children's author. Born Patricia Rubinstein, she wrote novels about the Marlow family and has been called "one of the finest writers of the 20th century" (*The Cambridge Guide to Children's Books in English*). She spent summer holidays with her mother's family in Bournemouth and moved to the town in 1938 on inheriting her aunt's house. Here she wrote ten books about the Marlow family at home and at school. She claimed that the gaps between her books were due to the need to work in her large garden.

Rejecting the Protestant faith of her Ulster mother and the Jewish faith of her Russian father, she became a Roman Catholic in 1947. Her unhappiness with the liturgical changes following the Second Vatican Council is conveyed in *The Attic Term* (1975). Her death was due to flu in a year in which three of her books were reprinted. She is believed to have destroyed her last uncompleted manuscript.

FORSE, Edward JG (c1880-1944), priest and author. In 1911 he was appointed Vicar of St Katharine's Church in Southbourne where he continued developing the catholic tradition, increased church income, edited a lively and much read parish magazine and founded a parish library. He travelled widely on the continent and gave popular lectures on his return from each trip. His sermons sometimes lasted 35 minutes. For the church's fiftieth anniversary in 1926 he wrote its history. In 1935 he reluctantly retired due to overwork but stayed in Southbourne by moving to Hollamby (since demolished) in Burtley Road opposite the church. This gave him time to complete his book *Ceremonial Curiosities and Queer Sights in Foreign Churches,* an account of festivals and liturgy illustrated with his own drawings, which was published in 1938. The church has a memorial plaque to him.

FORTE, Vincent (1906-1977), founder of Forte's in Bournemouth. He arrived in the town in 1937 on the day of his wedding attended by his cousin Charles (Lord Forte) who encouraged the romance and spent a year working at a local Forte's. Uncle Alfonso was already making ice cream in Swanage and Vincent and his wife Lilian, just a month after marrying, opened their own 'ice cream parlour' with an upstairs tea lounge. (It was destroyed by fire in 1993 and is now The Moon in the Square). In 1947 a Forte's restaurant seating 550 opened in a former dance hall (now The Brasshouse) in Westover Road. In 1968 Forte's took the ground floor of the new Royal London House at the Lansdowne. The following year the company was acquired by Lord Forte's Forte Holdings.

Lord Forte's son Rocco was born in Bournemouth.

FOX, Anthony Stoddart (1838-1905), founder of Fox & Sons estate agent. In 1868, having worked at a London estate agents, he set up his own in the capital. The venture was not a success and so the father of eight children went to manage a Hampshire country estate instead. When his son stayed in Bournemouth for his honeymoon in 1884 he saw the potential for an estate agency and persuaded his father to move to the town. In 1889 Anthony opened an office in Holdenhurst Road (Old Fire Station site). Four of his children joined the business including Lucy who remained the accountant until her death in 1934. There were branches at Westbourne and Southampton before younger son William opened new main offices in Old Christchurch Road, opposite Beales, in 1904. Anthony died the following year. After the First World War it fell to William to handle many land sales for Joseph Cooper Dean who succeeded his father James Cooper Dean* in 1921.

FOX, Charles (1921-1991), BBC Radio 3 broadcaster and jazz critic. He lived in Bournemouth from his mid teens to 1954, first working at Thomas Cook where he arranged the tickets for Ken Baily* and his team who 'ran' to America. During the Second World War Fox worked in the Experimental Bridging Establishment drawing office at Christchurch where Donald Bailey* was inventing the Bailey Bridge. After the war Fox played jazz records at Bournemouth Rhythm Club and, in the early Fifties, formed the Bournemouth Writers Group which met in his very untidy bedroom piled with records and magazines. Other members included the poet, and his lifelong friend, Christopher Logue.

FRY, Christopher (1907-2005), playwright, attended a pre-London performance at St Peter's Church of his play *A Sleep of Prisoners* specially written for the 1951 Festival of Britain. Over 3,000 people saw the previews.

FULLERTON, Lady Georgiana (1812-1885), author and philanthropist, first visited Bournemouth with her mother and later often stayed with her husband, Alexander Fullerton from Lymington, at Stewart's Hotel (now the Norfolk Royale Hotel) opposite the Sacred Heart Church where she worshipped for many years. Georgina was the daughter of Lord Granville, an ambassador, and as a child had sat on the Prince Regent's knee. She had piano lessons from Liszt and became a friend of Marie Antoinette's daughter. She also knew the prison reformer Elizabeth Fry. When in England Lady Georgiana stayed at Castle Howard or Chatsworth with her grandmother Georgina, Duchess of Devonshire.

In 1876 Lady Georgiana and her husband moved to Ayrfield (since demolished) in St Peter's Road. She had founded a convent (since demolished) in Branksome Wood Road and in 1873 opened St Joseph's Convalescent Home, adding in 1877 a school, at Blenheim (since demolished) on the north corner of Madeira and Lansdowne Roads. The former later moved to the convent and the latter moved to Avenue Road and in time became St Walburga's School in Moordown.

She always ensured that there were Christmas trees in the school and convent and she was responsible for introducing the custom to Menton in the south of France. She also wrote biographies, novels and books of verse. In 1884 her brother Lord Granville*, the Foreign Secretary, came from Osborne House by steamer to the pier on a visit. Her friends included Baroness von Hügel* and Sir Henry Taylor*.

She is commemorated with a plaque at the Church of the Sacred Heart, Bournemouth and in London's Farm Street Church. Her husband bought a house in the Via di San Sebastianello near the Spanish Steps in Rome for the Sisters of the Poor Servants and added the chapel in memory of Lady Georgiana. The convent has a sample of her hair in a silver case.

G

GALSWORTHY, John (1867-1933), author, playwright and Nobel Prize winner was a boarder at Saugeen School^ (Majestic Hotel site) in Derby Road from 1876 to 1881. He was escorted from home in Kingston-upon-Thames by his father's clerk Joseph Ramsden who was the model for Thomas Gradman in *To Let*, part of the *Forsyte Saga*. Galsworthy sang in the choir in the temporary St Swithun's Church building. In the *Forsyte Saga* he gave the name 'Swithin' to Jolyon's son. Bournemouth Pier, Branksome and its pines also feature. His sister recalled the "hot Sunday scent of the pines on the East Cliff" as she walked to church when visiting.

GENEEN, Harold (1910-1997), President ITT (International Telephone & Telegraph Corporation), one of the largest multinational conglomerates in the world which played a controversial role in toppling the Allende government in Chile, was born in Bournemouth shortly before his parents emigrated to America.

GEORGE V (1865-1936), as Prince George he accompanied his father the Prince of Wales (later Edward VII*) when he visited in 1890.

GEORGE VI (1895-1952), first British reigning monarch to visit Bournemouth when on 23 October 1941 he and Queen Elizabeth* inspected Dominion airmen at The Pavilion.

GEORGE, Charles (1846-1938), picture rail inventor who co-founded George & Harding. A building firm was established in 1867 by Charles George who bought land from Joseph Cooper Dean to erect houses in Lansdowne Road. That year he married Mary Miller at Christchurch Priory Church, set up home at number 29 (since demolished) on the northern corner of St Paul's Lane, and he met Henry Harding*. His works was behind the house and in 1883 he went into partnership with Harding building many houses, shop parades and familiar buildings including the Westbourne Hospital^, Bournemouth's Head Post Office and The Miramar Hotel. In 1898 the company rebuilt Brownsea Castle. On the corner of Lytton Road and Holdenhurst Road he built the George

Temperance Hall, a hotel for young men of the Band of Hope, as a gift.

In his forties, George suffered from tuberculosis and was given six months to live. Whilst staying in Madeira to avoid a British winter he invented a medicine to cure lung disease. On his return he bottled the mixture and sold it as George's Wonderful Patent Bournemouth Lung Healer and Blood Cleanser for at least the next twenty-five years whilst running his business, serving as a commissioner^, alderman and commanding officer of the volunteer corps.

GLADSTONE, William (1809-1898), Prime Minister. Towards the end of his life he arrived in Bournemouth on Tuesday 22 February 1898 to stay at Little Forest House (since rebuilt as flats) in Grove Road. He attended a Sunday afternoon children's service at St Swithun's Church where he sat under the pulpit so that he could hear. He made his last communion in a church at St Peter's kneeling in the choir stall so as to be near the altar rail but declining a hassock.

His stay lasted exactly a month and as he prepared to board the train home at Bournemouth East Station^ on Tuesday 22 March he said: "God bless you, and this place and the land you love." From the crowd came the cry: "God bless you sir!" He died at home in Wales two months later.

Among those in the small crowd at the station were five year old George England whose cousin Wallace Wait co-founded Waitrose and Ernest, son of Anthony Fox*. The Royal Bath Hotel, where Gladstone had stayed earlier, now has a Gladstone suite and there is Gladstone Road in Boscombe named after him.

GLOUCESTER, (Alice) Duchess of (1901-2004), wife of Duke of Gloucester*. In 1973 the Duchess visited Wallisdown to lay the foundation stone of the Bournemouth College of Technology which later became Bournemouth University. Her bodyguard was James Beaton who the following month was due to be assigned to newly married Princess Anne. Within four months he suffered an injury when he was shot during an attack on the Princess.

GLOUCESTER, Duke of (Henry) (1900-1974), son of George V. On a sunny March day in 1929 he laid a wreath at the war memorial in the Upper Pleasure Gardens and formally opened The Pavilion.

GODFREY, Sir Dan (1868-1939), conductor and pioneer of municipal music, moved from London to Bournemouth in 1893 to form and conduct a municipal band at the 4,000 seat glass Winter Gardens^ and provide outdoor music on the pier. The nucleus was the Royal Italian Band which had come to the town in 1876 for the winter and stayed. The Royal prefix was adopted after the band had been summoned to Crichel House to play at a ball given in honour of the Prince of Wales (later Edward VII*). Sir Dan Godfrey's first concert was on Whit Monday.

Symphony concerts began in 1895 with the band becoming the Bournemouth Municipal Orchestra the following year, a forerunner of the Bournemouth Symphony Orchestra inaugurated under his successor Sir Charles Groves*. Godfrey, who in 1911 also founded the Bournemouth Symphony Chorus, was admired by composer Charles Stanford. As early as 1908 Sir Edward Elgar wrote: "Godfrey has done so much for British music." The award of a knighthood for Godfrey himself in 1922 meant that the council felt obliged to maintain its level of funding.

In 1923 6BM, one of the country's first radio stations and part of the fledgling BBC, started broadcasting concerts conducted by Godfrey. Following one concert he suggested that listeners should "come to Bournemouth" to hear the orchestra live and afterwards was warned not to advertise. Being a council employee he was able to become President of the Bournemouth NALGO (now Unison) branch.

In 1922 he moved to Rosstrevor (now part of the Collingwood Hotel) on the Priory Road hill above the Winter Gardens. In 1925 his wife died. Four years later he became President of the Bournemouth Rotary Club and also married a widow, Annie Farlam. After his retirement in 1934 Godfrey lived at Danholme, 132 Alumhurst Road, which had a view of the Isle of Wight from the upstairs windows. He still rehearsed the orchestra but in 1937 suffered a stroke at the rostrum. He was helped by viola player Cedric Morgan who had just joined the orchestra and stayed until his own retirement until 1975. A large crowd stood outside St Peter's Church during Sir Godfrey's funeral. He is buried near the lych-gate.

GODWIN, William (1756-1836), philosopher and novelist, is buried with his wife Mary Wollstonecraft* in the Shelley tomb in St Peter's churchyard.

GOODALL, Sir Reginald (1901-1990), conductor and leading interpreter of Wagner who conducted world première of Britten's *Peter Grimes*, lived at 10 Luther Road in Winton. From 1940 to 1942 he conducted the Wessex Philharmonic Orchestra made up of former members of the Bournemouth Municipal Orchestra which had disbanded for the war. At his death tributes were marred by surprising and possibly unfair allegations that he had been a secret supporter of Hitler.

Sir Dan Godfrey's Band playing at Bournemouth

William Godwin, the father of Mary Wollstonecraft Shelley, is buried in the Shelley family tomb in St Peter's churchyard.
He and his wife Mary Wollstonecraft were reburied here from St Pancras churchyard.

Highcliff Hotel, Sir Alec Guinness's grandfather lived in the hotel grounds

East Cliff Cottage Hotel, Stewart Granger lived here as a child

GOUDGE, Elizabeth (1900-1984), prolific novelist, was a border during the First World War at Grassendale School (now St Peter's School) in St Catherine's Road where she claimed Jane Austen would have felt at home. Elizabeth's trips into the New Forest resulted in it being the setting for her book *The Eliots of Damerosehay*.

GOUGH, Hugh (1905-1997), Primate of Australia who made the Anglican Church independent of the Church of England, attended St John's Church, Boscombe and was a pupil at Gorse Cliff School (Gorsecliff site) in Boscombe Spa Road just before the First World War. He returned to the school as Bishop of Barking to present prizes shortly before becoming Archbishop of Sydney in 1958.

GRANGER, Stewart (1913-1993), actor, lived as a child at East Cliff Cottage (now a hotel) 57 Grove Road. A plaque on the house was unveiled in 1996 by his first wife Elspeth March and daughter Lindsay Granger.

GRANVILLE, Augustus Bozzi (1783-1872), Milan-born doctor who influenced the reputation of Bournemouth as a health resort, visited in 1841 by invitation of a group of residents eager to develop the village. He had just published volume I of his major work *The Spas of England and Principal Sea-Bathing Places*. He stayed in a new villa in Westover Road (Premier Lodge site) which was a very short walk from the (Royal) Bath Hotel where he was entertained to dinner by his hosts. Included in the party were probably Samuel Bayly* and John Sydenham*. He told his audience: "No situation that I have occasion to examine along the whole of the southern coast, possesses so many capabilities of being made the very first invalid sea watering place, but what is more important, a winter residence for the most delicate constitution requiring a warm and sheltered locality at this season of the year." Volume II of his guide devoted several pages to the emerging town.

GRAY, Charles (1928-2000), actor who played Blofeld in the 1971 James Bond film *Diamonds Are Forever*, lived for his first 23 years in Howard Road and attended Bournemouth School^ where he made his first stage appearance. His second was at the Palace Court Theatre^ whilst employed by Rebbeck's estate agent. He changed his name from Donald so as not to be confused with Donald Gray in the television series *Captain Scarlet*.

GREY, George (1809-1891), admiral and son of the Whig premier responsible for the 1832 Reform Bill, lived at Upton (now Abbey Mount Hotel) in Priory

Road which had been built in about 1867 for a former Rector of Downton, Richard Payne. But shortly afterwards it was occupied by another family who brought a butler and six staff. In 1875, shortly after moving there, the retired admiral was asked by Richard Potter to be a contact for his daughter Beatrice (Webb*) who was at boarding school.

GRIGG, Sir James (1890-1964), civil servant unexpectedly made Secretary of State for War in the Churchill* war cabinet. He was ten months old when his family moved from Exmouth to Bournemouth due to his carpenter father's work. He attended Bournemouth School^ from 1903 to 1908.

GROVES, Sir Charles (1915-1992), conductor, who in 1951 succeeded Rudolf Schwarz* as conductor of the Bournemouth Municipal Orchestra. Almost at once there was a crisis as audience numbers at the Winter Gardens^ fell and councillors called for cuts in funding. Groves is credited by many with saving the orchestra by fighting back. The following year, when Sir Alan Cobham* donated a car for a raffle, Groves stood in The Arcade selling tickets. £11,000 was raised and soon the Western Orchestral Society was formed to put the orchestra, now rebranded the Bournemouth Symphony Orchestra, on a better financial footing. The year after arriving he conducted the première of Malcolm Arnold's* Second Symphony and later championed his work even when unfashionable. In 1956 Groves took the BSO to London for its first performance at the Royal Festival Hall. He lived in Talbot Woods and was often seen collecting his two daughters from St Martin's School in Stoke Wood Road. In 1961 he left Bournemouth to become musical director of Welsh National Opera. He made a return visit as conductor in 1979.

GUINNESS, Sir Alec (1914-2000), Oscar-winning actor. He was the son of Bournemouth-born Agnes Cuff and his grandfather was a coastguard living in one of the cottages (in Highcliff Hotel grounds) and later Westbourne Arcade's caretaker. As a baby, Guinness was brought from London to play on the beach. He moved to the town when his mother married and settled in Southbourne where he attended Pembroke Lodge School (St Mary's Court site) in Belle Vue Road. The fees were paid by a banker, Andrew Geddes, who thought he was the child's father. The head teacher told Alec that he would never make an actor.

As he did not get on with his mother or step father he spent holidays with an uncle and aunt at Westbourne (Marks & Spencer site). At the age of 16 he wrote to Sybil Thorndike and was invited backstage to meet her and her husband Lewis Casson at The Theatre Royal^ in Albert Road which he called "a little old theatre" in a "damp little side street".

GULLIVER, Isaac (1745-1822), smuggler, moved in the early 1780s from Longham to be a wine and spirit merchant in Kinson. For a time he lived in Howe Lodge (demolished in 1958) in Brooke Road when he was still involved in landing contraband on the beach. His distribution network involved around two hundred well paid men. He returned to Kinson for about a year in 1815 living at Kinson House on the north-west corner of Horsham Avenue and Wimborne Road. (This site in the main road west of Kinson Grove is now flats.) He is remembered by Gulliver's Tavern which during his lifetime and until 1988 was known as The Dolphin.

GUSTAV VI (1882-1973), King of Sweden and grandson of Oscar II*, who visited the Russell-Côtes Museum & Art Gallery in 1977 accompanied by his granddaughter Princess Margaretha.

Thomas Hankinson

Marguerite Radclyffe Hall

Thomas Hardy

H

HALL, Radclyffe (1880-1943), poet and author of the first lesbian novel *The Well of Loneliness* which was banned for obscenity in 1928, was born at Sunny Lawn (now Durley Grange Hotel) in Durley Road to wealthy parents who called her Marguerite. Three weeks later her elder sister died. "Violent quarrels turned Sunny Lawn into a hell," she recalled and later referred to it in a poem starting "The sound of waves is the sound of tears". After three years, her father Radclyffe Radclyffe-Hall having left them, mother and daughter moved to London.

HAMEL, Gustav (1884-1914), pioneer aviator, broke the looping the loop record over Meyrick Park in 1914. A month later he disappeared whilst flying back to England over the English Channel.

HANCOCK, Tony (1924-1968), comedian, moved from Birmingham to Bournemouth in 1927 at the age of three with his parents and nanny. For a year they lived at 144 Strouden Road (since demolished) before his father Jack became landlord of The Railway Hotel (since demolished) on the western corner of Holdenhurst Road and St Paul's Road. The pub had a plaster frieze of fruit and was noted for its mahogany fittings. The chubby young Tony loved the fenced back garden.

As his father was an entertainer, appearing at such venues as St Peter's Hall and the Regent Theatre, he welcomed show business stars such as Charles Coburn who was famous for singing *The Man Who Broke the Bank at Monte Carlo*. The hotel's name may have inspired Tony's fictional East Cheam address 23 Railway Cuttings. Young Hancock briefly attended Summerbee Infants School (now Queen's Park Infants School) before going to Saugeen School^. Whilst a pupil he became a member of St Swithun's Church choir. In 1934 his parents bought The Swanmore Hotel (now The Quality Hotel) in Gervis Road. They renamed it Durlston Court Hotel after the Swanage school attended by their eldest son Colin. The following year Hancock's father died and Saugeen closed. In January 1936 Hancock was sent to the Swanage school where he remained until 1938. Just one year was spent at a Reading school before war broke out.

The day after, Hancock enrolled with Bournemouth Municipal College at The Lansdowne to learn shorthand and touch-typing. He also spent two weeks stamping ration books in the requisitioned Carlton Hotel. By then his show business aims had probably been inspired by the productions he saw at The Pavilion. In 1940 his mother approached George Fairweather as he finished his afternoon singing stint in Beales' restaurant and he agreed to help her son. Hancock's first appearance on stage since school was in 1940 at the Trades Union Club (now Avon Social Club) in Avon Road. Fairweather was organiser of concert parties for troops at the Theatre Royal^ in Albert Road and gave him a spot.

Less successful was Hancock's independent booking at the the Sacred Heart Hall on Richmond Hill where he was billed as 'Anthony Hancock - The Confidential Comic'. Troops were present but the 'saucy' material was still too strong for the audience who heard him in near silence. One of the organisers saw the 17 year old off at the door saying: "Thank you Mr Hancock, we won't require your services any further. We shall have to fumigate the stage." He took the advice of Fairweather never to tell blue jokes again and ended up running the troops' entertainment programme and appearing with George Fairweather at the Boscombe Hippodrome^.

In 1941 Jack Warner stayed at the Durlston Court Hotel whilst appearing at The Pavilion. Again Hancock's mother asked for help and Warner arranged for him to attend an audition in Bobby's restaurant (now Debenhams). This resulted in Hancock's first work with the BBC.

In 1942 he joined the RAF and was billeted at the Metropole Hotel (site of Royal London House) at the Lansdowne for almost two months. His mother's hotel was sold after the war but the 1962 film *The Punch & Judy Man*, starring Hancock playing a seaside entertainer, owes much to his memories of a Bournemouth childhood. In 1966 he appeared at the Winter Gardens^ for a week.

In 1984 a plaque on the Quality Inn Hotel was unveiled by his friend George Fairweather who then ran a hairdressing salon in Westover Road. The hotel now has a Hancock's Bar and Restaurant.

HANKINSON, Charles (1866-1959), author of *My Japanese Wife*, published in 1895, which he wrote under the name of Clive Holland, was born in Bournemouth where his father Thomas Hankinson* ran a library. His widely travelled son was awarded a knighthood for his writing by the King of Denmark. At home Hankinson opposed women's suffrage.

HANKINSON, Thomas James (1831-1905), first Mayor of Bournemouth, came from Norfolk with his wife Frances in 1858 to be the Branksome Estate land agent. He and his wife lived at Victoria House (the Moon in The Square site) in The Square. Soon he opened Hankinson's Victoria Circulating Library next door. The shop also sold books, stationery and wool. In 1865 he opened an estate agents which a decade later moved to its own premises at the bottom of Richmond Hill. This became Hankinson & Son when his youngest son Francis joined the business in 1888. Between 1876 and 1892 Thomas published local guide books. He was elected a Commissioner^ in 1873 and became chairman in 1876 which made him well placed to be invited to be the Charter Mayor in 1890. He was a Liberal Party member and a holder of several offices at Richmond Hill Congregational Church^. His elder son Charles Hankinson* was the author Clive Holland and his grandson Cyril edited *Debrett's Peerage*.

HARDING, Henry (1841-1915), plasterer and co-founder of George & Harding builders. His first job was on a farm but at the age of 20 he was apprenticed to a builder in Bournemouth. He met Charles George* in 1867 and two years later both joined the county Rifle Volunteer Corps. Harding had already built a line of houses on the west side of Oxford Road, close to George's works in St Paul's Lane, when in 1883 they formed George & Harding building and decorating contractors. On their land between Lansdowne and Oxford Roads they even had a nursery growing privet hedges for new gardens. The Harding family lived in one of the Oxford Road houses whilst George already lived in one he had built in Lansdowne Road at the opposite end of St Paul's Lane. Harding attended East Cliff Congregational Church in Holdenhurst Road where the nearby temperance Waverley Hotel was owned by the firm.

Charles George died in 1938 without an heir. In 2010 great grandson Colin Harding was chairman of G&H Group Ltd with board member Magnus Harding being the fifth generation to be involved in the business.

HARDY, Thomas (1840-1928), novelist, visited Bournemouth in 1875 soon after getting married. He was looking for somewhere to settle but chose to go to Swanage for some months instead where he wrote *The Hand of Ethelberta* in which Bournemouth figures as Sandbourne and Lord Malmesbury's* Hurn Court as the mansion. Sandbourne also features in *Tess of the D'Urbervilles.*

HARRIS of Greenwich, Lord (John) (1930-2001), Home Office minister and Police Foundation founder left school in Pinner in 1947 and joined the *Bournemouth Daily Echo* where his training was interrupted by National Service.

At the time he was 'Chancellor of the Exchequer' in the Bournemouth Model Parliament. By the time he was elevated to the peerage in 1974 his parents were living in Westbourne. He returned that year as a Home Office minister to pay an official visit to the Police Station in Madeira Road. Afterwards he went to Labour Hall^ to address his first Labour Party meeting since joining the government.

HART, Dame Judith (1924-1991), baroness and cabinet minister, was Bournemouth West Labour candidate in the 1951 General Election polling the highest vote of all her predecessors. During the campaign she lived in a cottage in West Way. As Paymaster-General she signed the visitors' book at the Mayor's Parlour in 1969 prior to being guest of the Socialist Ladies Luncheon Club at the Wessex Hotel. In 1977, as Minister of Overseas Development, she visited Beaufort School to speak in support of Joe Goodwin, Labour candidate in the Bournemouth East by-election caused by the resignation of John Cordle. There were only about 25 people there but she recalled that her 1951 Bournemouth adoption meeting was attended by 600 people and addressed by Colonial Secretary Jim Griffiths. In 1985 she attended a retirement party at The Pavilion for long-serving Labour councillor George Spicer who had helped her in 1951.

HATTS, Kenneth (1909-2007), artist, came to Bournemouth in the 1930s as a young illustrator and lived in St Swithun's Road whilst teaching at Bournemouth Municipal College of Art^. Among his early colleagues was Leslie Ward*.

After war service in India he returned to Bournemouth to live with his wife Betty first at Langtry House in Derby Road and from 1959 at 9 Stoke Wood Road. He was soon in demand for poster and leaflet design as paper restrictions were lifted. For many years he was responsible for the Bournemouth Symphony Orchestra's brochures and programme covers. As a pianist he enjoyed being allowed to sit in on rehearsals to sketch conductor Sir Charles Groves* in action. As a member of Holy Trinity Church^, Hatts was prevailed on to design and make a pair of modern outdoor notice boards for the Old Christchurch Road entrance. His efforts to find an alternative use for the building, such as a home for the BSO or the public library, failed when the church was declared redundant and later demolished.

Among his murals is one for Bowmakers (now a Bournemouth University building) in Christchurch Road and another featuring prehistoric life in the Dorset County Museum in Dorchester. In Bournemouth he worked with the architect Elizabeth Scott* by providing a ceiling design for the Pier café.

Post war colleagues at the college included John Liddell* with whom he worked closely as Chairman of the Bournemouth Arts Club. Hatts retired from the college, which had become the Bournemouth & Poole College of Art, in 1974 when he was Vice-Principal. Soon he illustrated a series of walks books written by his son Leigh including *Exploring The Bournemouth Coast Path*. In 1992, the Bournemouth Fabian Society's centenary year, he recast the national society's original tortoise logo designed by cartoonist Frank Horrabin. The new version remains in use and for more than a decade visiting speakers, including ministers and members of parliament, were presented with a mug bearing the tortoise.

In later years he specialised in flower paintings including one purchased by Ian Wooldridge* who predeceased him by three days. John Liddell's wife Joan Liddell* died on the same evening as Ken Hatts.

HAYLOCK, John (1918-2006), novelist who lived abroad to avoid being persecuted for his homosexuality, was born at Balsham 2 Clifton Road. His father was a doctor.

HEATH, Sir Edward (1916-2005), Prime Minister, was 11 when he cycled from his holiday home in Netley to hear the Bournemouth Municipal Orchestra under Sir Dan Godfrey*. Heath remained a supporter of the orchestra and in 1975 he conducted its successor, the Bournemouth Symphony Orchestra, at The Pavilion. This was a fund-raising event in the presence of Lord Mountbatten* and the conducting was shared with Rudolf Schwarz*. The soloist, with Heath at the rostrum, was Moura Lympany.

In 1979 he spoke at a Euro election meeting at the Town Hall. In 1987 he conducted a Summer Pops Concert at the Winter Gardens^ and in 1988 the Bournemouth Sinfonietta at the Royal Bath to mark the hotel's 150 anniversary. As well as sponsoring the BSO's principal flautist Karen Jones for three years he attended in 1991 a gala BSO concert at the Winter Gardens to raise funds. In 1993 he became President of the Bournemouth Gilbert & Sullivan Society. That year he addressed the Young Conservatives Conference on a Sunday morning at the Winter Gardens before lunching at the Palace Court Hotel^. During the 1998 Conservative Party Conference at the BIC^ he was photographed with Margaret Thatcher. However, by then he was living at Salisbury where he returned every night holding dinner parties for Tory friends who eagerly took the long taxi ride.

HEATH, Neville (1917-1946), murderer, fled to Bournemouth in June 1946 having murdered Margery Gardner in a London hotel and then, posing as 'George Armstrong', dined with actress Moira Lister*. He booked into the Tollard Royal Hotel (now Tollard Court flats) in St Michael's Road under the name 'Group Captain Rupert Brooke'. When out on a walk he met 19 year old Doreen Marshall who was staying at the Norfolk Hotel whilst recovering from illness. He attacked and killed her with a knife in Branksome Dene Chine leaving the body in rhododendron bushes. The knife was thrown into the sea as Heath washed away the blood. A search was started when the victim failed to return to the hotel and Heath was later arrested after getting off a bus where he had struck up a conversation with the young lady sitting next to him. "Never go out with strange men" he told the startled 18-year-old. He was charged at Madeira Road police station where earlier he had attempted to appear helpful when posing as 'Group Captain Brooke' and being interviewed by a sceptical detective George Suter. Heath was tried at the Old Bailey only for the first murder and hanged in the autumn.

HERBERT, 1st Baron Herbert of Lea (Sidney) (1810-1861), politician and friend of William Gladstone* lived at Eagles Nest (BIC^ Purbeck Hall site). Assisted by Florence Nightingale, he founded the Herbert Hospital at Charmouth which soon after his death was relocated as his memorial to purpose-built accommodation in Alumhurst Road at Westbourne.

HIGHT, Cecil (1918 -1940), Spitfire pilot shot down over Talbot Woods during the Battle of Britain in 1940, was the only allied airman to be killed over the town as a result of enemy action during the Second World War. He was hit by German machine gun fire and the aircraft crashed on the corner of Leven Avenue and Walsford Road. The young New Zealander had bailed out but was too injured to operate his parachute and fell to his death in a Leven Avenue back garden belonging to Alfred Hoare who saw the disaster. Headley Burrows* was in the area and went straight to the body. Four days later he presided at the burial in East Cemetery. Just three months later Alfred Hoare was killed when his house was bombed. In 1953 the New Zealand High Commissioner unveiled a plaque at St Peter's Church during a service broadcast live in New Zealand. Pilot Hight is also remembered by Pilot Hight Road in West Howe.

HILL, Benny (1924-1992), comedian, attended Bournemouth School for Boys for months from September 1839 as an evacuee from Southampton during the Second World War.

HOBLEY, McDonald (1917-1987), actor and early television announcer. Following a summer season in *Move Over, Mrs Markham* at the Pier Theatre in 1974, he bought a flat in the town. In 1981 he played the Demon in the *Mother Goose* pantomime at Poole Arts Centre. He died in Bournemouth.

HOLLAWAY, Antony (1928-2000), artist responsible for stained glass windows in Manchester Cathedral and a sculptural wall at Manchester University, was born in Kinson and studied drawing and painting at Bournemouth College of Art.

HOYLE, Sir Fred (1915-2001), astronomer who coined the term 'Big Bang', lived in retirement at Admiral's Walk in West Cliff Road from 1990.

Sir Henry Irving

South Bourne Terrace, Westover Road built by Henry Joy

I/J

IRVING, Sir Henry (1838-1905), actor, often visited Sir Percy Shelley* and stayed at the Royal Bath Hotel. He was also a guest of Sir Merton Russell-Côtes* at East Cliff Hall^. There Irving planted two ilex trees and another in the adjoining Royal Bath Hotel garden. He inaugurated the hotel's garden fountain during his final tour in 1905 which included the Grand Theatre^ at Boscombe where he played three nights and one matinee: *Conan Doyle's Waterloo*, *The Bells*, *Louis X1* and *The Merchant of Venice*. After his death Sir Merton bought many of his belongings which are now displayed in the Russell-Côtes Art Gallery & Museum.

JAMES, Colin (1926-2009), Bishop of Winchester, came to the town in 1967 after seven years as the BBC's Western Region Religious Broadcasting Organizer to be vicar of St Peter's Church. "The parish priest is the focal figure in the local church (i.e. the corporate life of the Christian community)," he once wrote. "He is not a one-man band. He is there for the people of God. And it is their parish, their church, and not his."

In 1970 he also took charge of St Stephen's Church which he loved and this was the beginning of the creation of the town centre parish which led to his successors at the mother church being rector rather than vicar. In 1973 he was appointed the first Bishop of Basingstoke and on the Sunday after his consecration as a bishop, but whilst still vicar, he entered St Peter's Church wearing a mitre to preside at the Eucharist.

In 1985, after serving as Bishop of Wakefield, he became the diocesan bishop at Winchester. He retired a decade later and at the time of his death was living with his Bournemouth-born daughter Harriet in Winchester.

JAMES, Henry (1843-1916), American author, lodged at a small hotel St Alban's (BIC^ site) from April to the end of June 1885 whilst completing *The Bostonians* and visiting Robert Louis Stevenson*. He returned the following year bringing him a mirror from Venice.

James stayed at the Royal Bath Hotel in 1897 finishing *What Maisie Knew*.

He once wrote: "Bournemouth has an almost American newness and ugliness. Its single saving grace was the view across to the Isle of Wight looking like a pretty marble toy on an ultramarine horizon."

JEFFERY-MACHIN, Ivor (1910-1985), priest and last vicar of Holy Trinity Church^, was a popular figure when he was appointed in 1967. He and his wife Brenda made a striking couple at the church and in the town. He bore a striking resemblance to his cousin the Chancellor of the Exchequer, James Callaghan. His wife dressed fashionably and wore very short skirts for her age and position as a former Mayor of Andover and vicar's wife. Both were supporters of the Bournemouth Symphony Orchestra and sat in the same seats at the Winter Gardens^ every Thursday.

Ivor was a catholic Anglican, although he respected Holy Trinity's low church tradition which he did not greatly seek to change. However, much to his distress the church closed in 1973. He was disgusted when the building was turned into a medieval style banqueting hall called King Arthur's Court. When in 1979 it burnt down in mysterious circumstances his reaction was: "Thank God, now I can walk past there in peace."

He had hoped to remain in the vicarage which, as a wealthy person through his wife's inheritance, he could afford to buy. However, the couple moved to Southbourne and the vicarage, childhood home of Anthony Blunt* and tennis star Virginia Wade, was demolished.

Ivor was very well-read and a Workers' Education Association tutor. In 1973 he won a round the world trip by appearing on ITV's National Knowledge Contest compered by Hughie Green. This success made the front page of the *News of the World* where it was noted that his name was so long (The Revd Canon Dr Ivor Jeffrey-Machin) that it stuck out over the end of the desk. Two years later he was a BBC Mastermind semi-finalist.

His funeral at St Peter's Church in 1985 was attended by James Callaghan*. Brenda died in 2003. The couple's bequest of almost a million pounds to the Workers' Educational Association resulted in the setting up of the Jeffrey-Machin Foundation to provide exciting and diverse learning opportunities for adults of all ages and backgrounds across Hampshire.

JEFFRIES, Lionel (1926-2010), actor who was starred in the film *Chitty Chitty Bang Bang* and directed *The Railway Children*, lived in Westbourne. He was proud that his great grandfather William Allison worked as a barber in The Square during the 1850s. He displayed an unofficial royal warrant on the grounds that he had cut the hair of Edward VII* when as Prince of Wales he was staying at the Royal Bath Hotel. Jeffries's grandmother also lived in the town. Although born in London he was named Lionel after an uncle living in Bournemouth. He attended Wimborne Grammar School. Actors and entertainers he worked with included Bob Hope, whom he once took to the Richmond Arms at Charminster near his mother's home. Jeffries was a familiar figure in the town and a supporter of the Dorset Wildlife Trust among other causes. He died in a Poole nursing home.

JENKINS, Roy (1920-2003), cabinet minister, was guest speaker at the Fabian Society dinner at The Pavilion in 1976 when he had ceased to be Home Secretary for the second time and had just left the House of Commons. He felt "it was imperative" to come as he had been unable to keep his earlier two promises to visit - once due the Birmingham bombings. During his speech he reflected that it was his last address before leaving the Labour movement to become European Commission President. He considered his appointment as being more important than any government office other than the premiership. "It's the most difficult challenge in my life and that includes my years as Chancellor," he added.

JOHNSON, Amy (1903-1941), pioneer aviator. In order to recover from a nervous breakdown she stayed in October 1925 for five weeks with her father's cousins the Eddison family in Kinross Road. Later Amy took up flying and in 1930 flew solo to Australia. Afterwards, during a tour of seaside towns sponsored by the *Daily Mail*, she landed near Talbot Village and, having opened a fête at Meyrick Park, was guest of honour at a civic reception hosted by the Mayor, Alderman Percy Bright, son of Frederick Bright*.

JOHNSON, Thomas Lewis (1836-1921), a slave for 28 years in Virginia, moved to Bournemouth in 1895 with his wife Sarah. He had visited in 1893 after having knee problems and used a bath chair whilst convalescing. On returning the following year to conduct a mission at St John's Church Boscombe, at the invitation of vicar SA Selwyn, Johnson decided to live in the town. His home was Liberia 66 Paisley Road where he displayed slave chains and whips. He became a familiar object of interest as a rare black man. "Shake hands. The black won't come off!" he said to people in the street. In 1900 he became a British subject.

His autobiography *Twenty-eight Years a Slave*, which ran to seven editions, was jointly published by W Mate & Sons of Bournemouth and Christian Workers Depot.

JONES, Alfred (c1826-1916), founder of 'scientific bootmakers' A Jones & Sons. Alfred and Emma Jones started the footwear chain in London in 1857 specialising in readymade shoes in three sizes. The shop was at first best known for having electric light. Eventually, with all their nine sons being encouraged to open a shop on their own, the company's slogan was, "Each branch managed by a member of the family." In 1883 the parents retired to their Bournemouth home Denbigh Lodge, 64 Surrey Road. However, the following year Alfred opened a shop (Debenhams site) in The Square. Later sons Edgar and Edward took over this business and in 1909 the shop moved to its present address in Gervis Place.

JONES, Benjamin (1848-1947), leading co-operator who knew the Rochdale Pioneers and was co-author of the influential *Working Men Co-operators* (1883) and *Co-operative Production* (1894), resigned as CWS London Manager in 1902 to buy The Queen's Hotel (now Jacey House) at The Lansdowne. He also ran a bakery and three beach cafés. It was at his suggestion that the cafés eventually became municipal enterprises. In 1903 he founded the Bournemouth Bowls Club and in 1906 was the first President of the Bournemouth & District Bowling Association. He was a life member of the Queen's Park Golf Club. He was visited at his home Bens Holme cottage (since demolished) next to the Tuckton Toll Bridge by Beatrice Webb*.

JONES, John Daniel (1865-1942), Congregational minister and Honorary Secretary of the Congregational Union, was Minister of Richmond Hill Congregational Church^ from 1898, soon after the building was completed, until 1937. By his personality and preaching he and his church became so well-known that the International Congregational Council agreed to meet in Bournemouth in 1930. He was instrumental in founding the non-conformist school which became Wentworth College. On his retirement he was granted the freedom of the borough.

JONES, Spencer (1857-1943), priest and co-founder of the annual Week of Prayer for Christian Unity. In a letter written to Father Paul Wattson of New York which triggered the idea, Jones mentions being in Bournemouth "last week". This was around 5 November 1907 when with his wife, a relative of John Keble*, he visited the new Keble Chapel at St Peter's Church. Jones was much preoccupied with the lack of dialogue between Anglicans and Roman Catholics and on returning home to Moreton-in-Marsh proposed an annual day of prayer for unity which became a week.

JOY, Henry (1822-1906), carpenter and builder, moved to Bournemouth in 1849. His first project was South Bourne Terrace, the parade of shops which includes WH Smith, completed in 1863. Three years later he began to construct The Arcade over Church Glen which had been crossed on the same site by a rustic bridge built of pine logs in 1853. This bridge had a halfpenny toll and spanned the valley with a stream running down from Horseshoe Common to join the Bourne near The Square. The Old Christchurch Road end was opposite two thatched cottages. Regret at the loss of this attractive amenity led local people to call the new arcade 'Joy's Folly'. Now a town commissioner^, he lived at Seymour House (Eldon Place site) in Westbourne where in 1884 he built the adjacent arcade. The house gave its name to Seymour Crescent which is part of the one-way system.

Joy was able to proceed with the arcade plan despite having been successfully sued in previous year in the Royal Courts of Justice in London for breach of engagement. The widowed but recently remarried Joy was accused by Mrs Eleanor Miller who had been briefly manageress of the Queen's Hotel (now Jacey House) at The Lansdowne. She alleged that he had entered her bedroom on a Sunday morning whilst she was in bed and on another occasion given her a ring. Joy appears not so much to have feared the lurid press coverage but that the case would expose him as not being as rich a man as people in Bournemouth believed him to be.

He died at home Duncairn (Adelphi Court site) in Manor Road.

John Keble

Brookside, John Keble's house in Exeter Lane

K

KEBLE, John (1792-1866), priest, hymn writer and author of *The Christian Year* who initiated the Church of England's catholic revival, came to Bournemouth on 11 October 1865 after retiring as vicar of Hursley. Keble and his sick wife Charlotte booked into "an inconvenient lodging". Two weeks later they found Brookside (The Hermitage Hotel grounds) in Exeter Lane and by January Keble was happy to write, "We do not at all repent of having come here." He walked daily across the gardens and over the River Bourne to attend the Eucharist at St Peter's Church where he had once preached and knew the vicar Morden Bennett*. He also worshipped at St Swithun's Church. During the last six months of his life he corresponded with such leading Oxford Movement figures as William Gladstone*, John Henry Newman and Dr Edmund Pusey. He was also involved in preparations for the publication of his Oxford lectures. Keble's sister-in-law Bessie stayed to help nurse his wife. He died at Brookside early on Maundy Thursday 29 March. His wife died in May. The following year he was depicted in a stained glass window in St Peter's Church south transept which since 1906 has been known as the Keble Chapel. St Stephen's Church, built shortly after his death, was placed under the patronage of his memorial Keble College, Oxford. He is commemorated on 14 July in the Anglican calendar.

KEMAL, Ali (1869-1922), the Ottoman Empire's last interior minister who was assassinated for opposing Mustafa Kemal Ataturk, accompanied his wife Winifred in 1909 when she gave birth to their son Osman at Ravello 8 Lorne Park Road. This was the home of her mother Margaret Brun. Soon Winifred died and Kemal returned to Turkey leaving his baby in the care of Margaret. Eventually Osman, taking his grandmother's maiden name, became Wilfred Johnson. His son Stanley was elected as a British MEP and the grandson Boris became Mayor of London.

KEMP-WELCH, Lucy (1869-1958), artist and illustrator of Anna Sewell's *Black Beauty,* was born in a terraced house on Poole Hill. Later, home was Dinmore just beyond County Gates. Lucy drew beetles for her father, a solicitor and entomologist, and enjoyed studying nature in the New Forest. She was educated at home until the age of nine before attending Towerfield School (now closed) near Pine Tree Glen in Poole Road. Her next school in Poole discouraged her art but in 1883 at the age of fourteen she exhibited publicly for the first time. In 1891 she and her sister Edith*, having attended Drummond Road School of Art^, were both accepted for Herkomer School of Art at Bushey in Hertfordshire. She became famous in 1895 with her *Gypsy Horse Drovers* painting now in Russell-Côtes Art Gallery and Museum. She lived in Watford but often returned home. In 1925 she became Vice-President of the Bournemouth Arts Club and at its 1930 exhibition at Poole Hill College, 45 Poole Hill (now Bumbles) she showed *Mixed Company at a Race Meeting*.

KEY, Gwynneth (1911-2010), Headmistress of Bournemouth School for Girls, became 'BSG' headmistress in 1946 when the school was on the corner of Meyrick Road and Gervis Road behind the Municipal College. She retired in 1976 after overseeing the move to the present site in East Way in 1960. She had known Michael Foot at Oxford and like him was a Labour Party member. She was, like her predecessor Edith Burras, a keen supporter of the United Nations Association. She was also the local president of the Historical Association and in 1948 visited Germany to lecture history teachers. She had considerable influence beyond her school as President of the Six Counties Branch of the Head Mistresses' association and a member of the county borough education committee. Around 400 past pupils attended her farewell as headmistress.

KILVERT, Francis (1840-1879) priest and diarist, visited Bournemouth in December 1875. His diary entries for this period are lost but a later passage looking back refers to snow, pine trees and "sand hills on the East Cliffe and in Boscombe Chine". His stay may have been for reasons of health as he was often ill.

KING, Dr Horace (1901-1986), Speaker of the House of Commons. In 1930 he became Head of English at Taunton's School in Southampton and on the outbreak of war in September 1939 moved with the school to Bournemouth School for Boys' new buildings in East Way. The evacuated school arrived ahead of the local boys who were still at the old site in Porchester Road. Whilst in Bournemouth he addressed one of the Bournemouth Fabian Society's Sunday afternoon meetings at The Wilderness, on the south corner of Wimborne Road and St Valerie Road, home of Dr Ernest Seeley. He also entertained troops in town. In 1973, as Lord Maybray-King, he told the Junior Chamber of Trade at The Carlton Hotel that it was one of the glories of

British democracy that people could be politically opposed and yet be personal friends.

KNIGHT, Cyril (1908-1982), composer and organist, succeeded Percy Whitlock* in 1936 as organist at St Stephen's Church. The choir benefited greatly when Knight recruited boys for the choir from Porchester School where he taught music. He stepped down in 1966 due to a lack of choirboys and became organist at St Peter's Church. He returned to St Stephen's Church in 1976 and stayed until a month before his death. He was also Chorus Master of The Municipal Choir. *The New English Hymnal* includes his tune *Meyrick Park* which he composed for Charles Wesley's hymn *With solemn faith we offer up*.

Lillie Langtry

L

LANG, Matheson (1879-1948), Canadian actor who first toured America with Lillie Langtry*, was playing in *The Wandering Jew* at The Pavilion in December 1936 when the cast gathered on stage to hear Edward VIII's abdication broadcast. A radio was placed on top of a beer crate. Lang's cousin was the Archbishop of Canterbury Cosmo Gordon Lang who had been involved the crisis talks regarding the abdication.

LANGTRY, Lillie (1853-1929), actress who gave her name to Langtry USA. The beautiful daughter of the Dean of Jersey was drawn into the London season in April 1876 when one of her earliest acquaintances was Lord Wharncliffe, a colleague of Bournemouth's MP Sir Henry Drummond Wolff*, remembered by Wharncliffe Road.

Her first visit to Bournemouth was in 1877 to stay with Lord Malmesbury* at Hurn Court where she fished in the River Stour. A young gardener, who asked to give her a magnolia blossom, noted that her skin resembled the flower. Whilst at the house, she wrote an indiscreet note to the Prince of Wales (later Edward VII*). After her suspicious husband held up the blotting pad to the mirror and read the letter, Malmesbury gave strict instructions to the staff to renew blotting paper regularly.

At dinner he asked her if the soup was to her liking and she replied that it would be even better hot. The Earl quickly tasted it and scalded his mouth whilst she fell about laughing. He gave her old prints which she hung in her London home.

That year, under the name of 'Emilie Langton' she started building The Red House (now Langtry Manor Hotel) in Derby Road which was allegedly financed by the Prince of Wales. The builder was William Hoare who later became Mayor and whose Victoria Works was nearby on the south corner of Holdenhurst and Wellington Roads. The fireplace in the main bedroom of the Langtry Manor Hotel is decorated with tiles depicting scenes from Shakespeare's plays and was probably designed by Frank Miles who had sketched Lillie. Edward is believed to have visited her there and the curtain ties featured the Prince of Wales' feathers. Over the gallery are written the words: "They say, What say they? Let them say."

Lillie, who kept up an intimate correspondence with an old flame in Jersey, retreated to the house in 1881 with her baby Jeanne-Marie whose father was allegedly Prince Louis Battenberg. The birth, which took place in Paris, is commemorated in a window dated 1881 on the stairs.

Lillie built Langtry House in the grounds for her own mother and there grandmother and child lived whilst Lillie launched her acting career and endorsed Pear's Soap. She travelled by train to Wimborne and then by carriage to Crichel House when the Prince of Wales was a guest there. The Red House was rented out on Lillie's departure for her first American tour in 1882. A year later she returned briefly and again in 1886-7 before the house was sold in 1892. Mrs Langtry appeared in The Crossways at the Boscombe Hippodrome^ but in 1906 she cancelled an appearance at the Winter Gardens^ at short notice.

LAWLER, Sylvia (1922-1996), human geneticist and first female professor at Institute of Cancer Research, was born Sylvia Corben at 33 St Clement's Road. She attended Wentworth College where she was the first pupil to study medicine. The Sylvia Lawler Prize is administered by the Royal Society of Medicine.

LAWRENCE, DH (1885-1930), author, arrived in January 1912 at Compton House boarding house (Mercury House site) in St Peter's Road. "I advise you never to come here for a holiday" he wrote to his fiancée Jessie Chambers. "The place exists for the sick. They hide the fact as far as possible, but it's like a huge hospital. At every turn you come across invalids being pushed or pulled along." He was struck by the dark pine trees and the golden cliffs and, being winter, he enjoyed watching the waves breaking across the promenade.

His enforced visit was due to the need to recover from double pneumonia which had nearly killed him and ended his teaching career. There were the distractions of older residents wanting to talk and pretty girls, but over a month he worked for about two hours a day rewriting *The Trespasser* at the request of his publisher. His advice to his fiancée not to visit may have been due to his intention to break off the engagement.

LAWSON, George Joseph (1852-1936), builder, came to Bournemouth on his honeymoon and stayed. In the pine woods east of the present station he set up a general joinery and building works which included a steam saw mill. He was a deacon in the Congregational Church who oversaw (and probably designed) the building of the East Cliff Congregational Church which opened in 1879 on the site of a cattle pound. He was the superintendent of its Sunday school for many years and his wife was the church's first woman deacon.

Boscombe Arcade built by George Lawson

The Earls of Levin & Melville owned and developed the Talbot Woods estate

In 1882 he formed a partnership with London architect John Donkin. Over the next few years Lawson & Donkin was responsible for Granville Chambers and the Empress Hotel, both temperance hotels, on Richmond Hill and the nearby Richmond Hill Congregational Church^. In Boscombe they built the Grand Continental Arcade and adjoining Grand Pavilion Theatre^ which opened in 1892-3. This music hall was so controversial that a rival builder added the figure of the devil on the building opposite in 1896. In 1910-11 Lawson built the Synagogue in Wotton Mount.

As Mayor in 1901 he read the proclamation announcing the accession of Edward VII before a large crowd in The Square. At the time the town hall was a Lawson building in Yelverton Road. For about 15 years his home was at 2 Southcote Road which displays his initials GJL on the frontage.

LEES, Dodo (Dolores) (1920-1991), war heroine who was awarded the Croix de Guerre, crossed German lines to take food to allies and lived in a cave. As a young journalist she met Hitler with whom she shared a birthday. He wrongly predicted that she would do well in politics although in 1950, as a member of the Lees of Lychett Minster family, she was well placed to be the feisty Labour candidate for Bournemouth East & Christchurch against Brendan Bracken*.

LENNOX-BOYD, Alan (1st Viscount of Merton) (1904-1983), Colonial Secretary, was born at Loddington 13 Knole Road (now Boscombe Grange Hotel). His father spent much time away so his mother, his father's second wife, had a strong influence on him. As an MP and cabinet minister he returned to the town, where his sister continued to live and worship at Holy Trinity Church^, for the 1955 Conservative Conference.

LEVEN & MELVILLE, 11th Earl of Leven & 10th Earl of Melville (1835-1906), Lord Keeper of the Privy Seal of Scotland and banker to Mary Anne Talbot*, inherited the Talbot sisters' estate on the death of Mary Anne. His memorial to her is Talbot Manor (just inside the old county boundary in Talbot Avenue) built in 1890 for destitute boys and is now a Shaftesbury Society residence.

He allowed cycling in Talbot Woods but banned cars and dogs. Smoking was forbidden in the woods due to the fear of bracken catching fire. He donated the land for Winton Library, the town's first purpose built library, which opened the year after his death. His wife was Emma Portman, granddaughter of the 1st Viscount Portman*.

LEVEN & MELVILLE, 12th & 11th Earl of (1886-1913), succeeded his father the 11th & 10th Earl* at the age of twenty in 1906. He died at the early age of 27 following a hunting accident in Scotland.

LEVEN & MELVILLE, 13th & 12th Earl of (1890-1947), succeeded his brother 12th & 11th Earl* at the age of 23 in 1913. He developed Talbot Woods as a residential area and in 1921 donated 194 acres to enlarge Meyrick Park. Five years later he gave the Pug's Hole to the town. Leven Avenue runs alongside Meyrick Park and there is a Melville Road in Winton. Glenferness Avenue is named after the family's Scottish home at Nairn.

LIDDELL, Joan (1925-2007), artist and President of the British Migraine Association, trained as a textile designer at Hornsey College of Art where she met her husband John Liddell*. Both taught at the Bournemouth College of Art. When pushing her son Adam in the pram she would see her near neighbour Gerald Durrell* with a chimpanzee in a pram. She was an active member of the British Migraine Association and succeeded its founder Peter Wilson first as Secretary and in 1981 as Director. In 1997 she was the first Honorary President. She produced screen prints and watercolours of mainly flowers and plants in her garden at 90 Richmond Park Avenue. By 2001 she was too ill, following a series of strokes, to receive in person the World Headache Alliance's Elizabeth Garrett Anderson Award.

LIDDELL, John (1924-2005), printmaker and grandson of the Edwardian painter Rosa Braithwaite, moved from Wallingford in 1954 to be head of Education at Bournemouth College of Art where the principal was wood engraver Fred Courtney. Other colleagues were etcher Frank Dodman, painter John Spencer and graphic designer Ken Hatts*. The Liddell prints, often single block in black ink, began to feature Poole Quay as well as Devon villages and Norfolk churches. At the college he acted as slide and film projectionist assisting visiting lecturers such as David Hockney, Reg Butler and Alan Bowness. In 1979, when his department was abolished, John left the college and continued to teach elsewhere part time. He was also a leading member of the Bournemouth Arts Club. His home 90 Richmond Park Avenue, shared with his wife Joan Liddell*, was a large Victorian house packed with his prints. An old press stood in the front room. In 1991 he founded Poole Printmakers in an old warehouse in Bowling Green Alley off the High Street where he ran courses and operated old hand presses.

LISTER, Moira (1923-2007), actress who met Neville Heath* just before he murdered for a second time. She stayed at the Normandie Hotel for a week in 1981 when last appearing at the Poole Arts Centre.

LOUISE, Princess (Duchess of Argyll) (1848-1939), Queen Victoria's daughter in 1863 sailed from the Isle of Wight to the pier to visit the Queen's doctor Sir James Clark*. The 15 year old girl dined at his home Eagle's Nest in Exeter Road (BIC^ entrance site) and visited Cranborne Gardens, also called Archery Grounds (now the Winter Gardens^), and the coastguard cottages (now in the grounds of the Highcliff Hotel) where she admired the view. The Princess returned in 1903 to open a children's ward at Westbourne Hospital^ when visiting Lord Malmes-bury* at Hurn Court. Her father-in-law the 8th Duke of Argyll* had fond memories of the town.

LOWRY, Somerset C (1855-1932), priest and composer whose work includes the hymn *Son of God, eternal Saviour,* was curate of Holy Trinity Church^ from 1884 to 1890 and in 1900 he succeeded fellow hymn writer Henry Twells* as Vicar of St Augustin's Church. He left in 1911 but returned to the town in 1919 to live at 14 Madeira Road (site of Coppen Court).

LUSH, Ernest (1908-1988), piano accompanist on early radio who played for Kathleen Ferrier, was born in Bournemouth and attended Bournemouth School (then in Porchester Road). In 1923, when an evening lecturer failed to arrive on time, Lush stepped in to play popular songs on the piano. He studied in London at the age of 15 and in 1927 returned to make his solo debut with the Bournemouth Municipal Orchestra.

LYMPANY, Moura (1916-2005), Second World War concert pianist, was playing in Bournemouth with the wartime Wessex Philharmonic Orchestra when a bomb could be heard exploding at Southbourne. The conductor of Beethoven's Fourth Piano Concerto, however, brought the orchestra in on time and she described this as the most exciting moment of her career. That evening while at the home of Leslie Bickel in Queen's Park she had to throw herself on the floor for safety when bombs fell nearby.

M

MACDONALD, George (1824-1905), Scottish novelist and poet, lived at Boscombe in a house surrounded by pine trees (in St John's Road area) from 1875 to 1877. He was already well-known for his unorthodox views and preached at the Congregational Church. Sir Percy Shelley* went to hear him in September 1877 just two months before MacDonald left the town. During this period he wrote *Sir Gibbie* which was published in 1879.

MACDONALD, Ramsay (1866-1937), first Labour Prime Minister, was present in 1926 at the TUC meeting at the Town Hall and addressed the Bournemouth Labour Party and Independent Labour Party rally at the Drill Hall (now flats) in Holdenhurst Road. In 1929, he attended the opening of the Labour Hall^ (rebuilt as Lincoln Hall flats) in Lincoln Avenue. It was just before the General Election and he told the party members: "We expect great things of you in Bournemouth, and also your candidate, Colonel Maurice Spencer." The Bournemouth candidate lost but MacDonald returned to Downing Street in June after a five year gap filled by Stanley Baldwin.

MACGREGOR, John (1825 -1892), Rob Roy canoe inventor and author of Rob Roy books including *A Thousand Miles in a Rob Roy Canoe,* spent his last years at Lochiel in Wharncliffe Road where he died.

MACMILLAN, (Maurice) Harold (1894-1986), Prime Minister, stayed as Foreign Secretary at The Carlton Hotel during the 1955 Conservative Party Conference held at The Pavilion. On his 85th birthday in 1979 he returned to spend a night at the East Cliff Court Hotel prior to addressing the Young Conservative National Conference at the Winter Gardens^ where he received a five minute standing ovation. The Labour government was coming to an end and the new Conservative Leader Margaret Thatcher had already spoken at the gathering. He ended his speech by saying: "In the coming election you must appeal to those with the highest instincts, the maximum of people of moderate opinion in this year of the election while we older ones stand back. I pray God's blessings on you all." Excerpts were used in a televised Conservative party political broadcast.

MALMESBURY, 1st Earl of (1746-1820), diplomat, MP for Christchurch and son of philosopher James 'Hermes' Harris. In 1795, the year after Malmesbury negotiated the Prince Regent's engagement to Princess Caroline, whom he described as "stocky, jutting and malodorous", he inherited Hurn Court from his unmarried cousin Edward Hooper. The partly 15th-century house had been the country residence of the Priors of Christchurch. Malmesbury, who had been ennobled in 1788, was raised to an earldom in 1800. He soon owned a large area of Bournemouth partly due to the awards following the 1802 Christchurch Enclosure Act. Malmesbury Park Road recalls the ownership, Fitzharris Avenue takes its name from his eldest son's courtesy title Lord Fitzharris and Orcheston Road is derived from Orcheston St George in Wiltshire where the family once lived.

Smugglers' wagons from the coast were to be seen clattering past the house in the 1790s. In 1809 (probably at the instigation of his son the future 2nd Earl* who spent more time at Hurn) Labrador dogs, then known as St John's dogs, arrived from Newfoundland which had strong links with the nearby Poole.

MALMESBURY, 2nd Earl of (1778-1841), a sportsman who devoted his life to the estate changed its name from Hurn Court to Heron Court. A rhododendron forest he planted lasted until being destroyed by fire in 1934. He continued his father's interest in St John's (Labrador) dogs by starting a kennels for the new breed. In 1834 he laid the foundation stone of the present Holdenhurst church which was to replace the Saxon building.

MALMESBURY, 3rd Earl of (1807-1889), Foreign Secretary, witnessed smugglers hiding kegs of brandy on his Hurn (Heron) Court estate when a child. His guests included Lord Palmerston* who rode over from his home Broadlands near Romsey and Lillie Langtry*. In May 1884 the estate was the source for hawthorn and lilac in the bedroom of the sick Lady Georgina Fullerton* in central Bournemouth. He continued the family interest in St John's dogs and in 1887 helped to further establish their new name by referring to them as Labradors when writing to the Duke of Buccleuch. Labrador is the Canadian territory near Newfoundland where they had originated and the name had already been used by Edward Landseer when painting a dog. In 1873 the Earl laid the foundation stone of the present St John's Church Moordown. He and his wife enjoyed plays at the home of Sir Percy Shelley*. Today Lord Malmesbury's portrait hangs in a Foreign Office room overlooking Downing Street.

The 1st Earl of Malmesbury

The 3rd Earl of Malmesbury

MALMESBURY, 5th Earl of (1872-1950), last Malmesbury to live at Hurn (Heron) Court which from 1935 he called by this original name. He inherited in 1899 and was visited by Princess Louise* in 1903 and twice by Kaiser Wilhelm* in 1907. During the Second World War the mansion became a Red Cross headquarters. He was President of the Library Association when it held its first national conference in Bournemouth in 1949. The following year he sold the contents of his own 47 foot long, 26 foot wide library and moved to Winchester where he died two months later.

MALMESBURY, Sylvia, Countess of (1855-1934), wife of 4th Earl, lived from 1899 as Dowager Countess at Throop House which was built in 1807 but has a much older thatched cob wall alongside the Throop-Holdenhurst road.

MARCONI, Guglielmo (1874-1937), Italian inventor, Nobel Prize winner and radio pioneer, set up a wireless transmitter at the Madeira Hotel (now Court Royal Hotel) on the West Cliff in January 1898. After a few months he moved downhill to next door Sandhills (since demolished) where he signalled to Swanage. At Bournemouth he received the first paid radiogram which had been sent from his station on the Isle of Wight. In September, when the lease expired, he moved the equipment to the Haven Hotel at Sandbanks. In later years his yacht could be seen sailing off the coast.

MARGARET, Princess (1930-2002), sister of Elizabeth II, visited in 1972 at her own request the Royal National Hospital arriving by train and lunching at The Carlton Hotel. In 1988 she arrived by train to lunch with the Mayor and visit Epiphany School at Muscliff and in June 1994 she visited the Retired Nurses National Home in Riverside Avenue to mark its diamond jubilee.

MARIE AMÉLIE THÉRÈSE (1782-1866), Queen of France and widow of Louis Philippe, lived in 1862 at Albert House (Theatre Royal^ site) with its grounds covering the present Yelverton Road.

MARIE LOUISE, Princess (1872-1956), granddaughter of Queen Victoria, often stayed at The Carlton Hotel with her sister Princess Helena Victoria. Once there was panic at the hotel when a jewel box did not appear in their rooms with the luggage. It was found to have fallen off their car roof rack in Surrey and been handed to the police by a passing motorcyclist. On another occasion Princess Helena Victoria's knitting went missing but that was found left in the car. In 1919 Princess Marie Louise was entertained to tea by Lady Russell-Côtes at East Cliff Hall^.

The Carlton's manager and his wife were invited by Princess Marie Louise to Princess Helena Victoria's funeral at Windsor.

MARIE VALERIE (1868-1924), Archduchess of Austria, stayed at Royal Exeter Hotel with her mother Empress Elizabeth* in 1888. The Archduchess took a carriage to Southbourne and Christchurch. On Sunday she attended the 8 a.m. Mass at the Church of the Sacred Heart. The following year her brother Crown Prince Rudolf died mysteriously with his lover at Mayerling.

MARTYN, Charles (1917-1999), the Queen's hairdresser from 1968 to 1997, lived in Westbourne and attended Her Majesty weekly. When travelling abroad they enjoyed doing crosswords together. On his retirement, two years before his death, he was made a Member of Royal Victorian Order. His funeral was at Hinton Admiral Church where the Queen was represented by Woman of the Bedchamber Mary Morrison.

MAYO, Arthur (1840-1920), was awarded VC at age of 17 for leading a charge during the Indian Mutiny in 1857. He retired in 1901 to live with his youngest daughter Margaret at Guiliano 23 Rosebury Road. He was unusual in being ordained deacon in the Church of England whilst becoming a Roman Catholic layman. Three sons were Jesuit priests so he was pleased to be able to attend nearby Corpus Christi, a Jesuit church, where from 1911 to 1915 he was organist and choirmaster. He had a good singing voice and was an expert in plainsong. He died at home in 1920 on his 80th birthday. Son Raymond celebrated the funeral Mass in the presence of his other sons and brother, Anglican Canon Edward Mayo. Having served with 4th Indian Naval Brigade he was buried in Bournemouth East Cemetery with full naval honours. A memorial stained glass window was installed in Corpus Christi Church.

McNESS, Frederick (1892-1956), VC, was decorated for leading a counter attack against the Germans in 1916 in France although severely wounded. He was at once promoted to Sergeant in the 1st Battalion Scots Guards. On his retirement he moved from Leeds to a bungalow at 37 Petersfield Road in January 1956. In May he committed suicide whilst his wife was out. His ashes were scattered in Bournemouth's North Cemetery Garden of Remembrance. A painting of him in action hangs at Wellington Barracks in Birdcage Walk, London.

MEARS, Harry (1892-1987), Mayor and Cinema Exhibitors Association founder member, arrived in Bournemouth in 1929 on his doctor's advice. Suffering from a respiratory problem and just married, he stayed in Winton where he discovered the Electric Palace Cinema (Hop and Kilderkin site). He soon purchased the building, designed by John Fogerty*, and renamed it first The Plaza and later The Continental. This became well-known for its X rated films and was the country's oldest private cinema when it closed in 1989. Other local cinemas were soon under his ownership or management. He was elected councillor for Winton in 1936 and was Mayor in Coronation year 1953 and again a decade later. This was followed by a third term due to his successor's illness. During the Second World War he was in charge of ARP wardens and civil defence. Post-war as chairman of six council committees he was the most powerful and feared politician. His nickname was 'Tiger' because of his tenacity.

Towards the end of his life he opposed the building of the BIC^ (Bournemouth International Centre). He lived outside the town in West Moors and also in Christchurch, even when Mayor, but in 1967 he moved to Ocean Heights in Boscombe Cliff Road. His wife Hilda, before coming to Bournemouth, formed the first all women's band and enjoyed motorcycling.

MERRY DEL VAL, Raphael (1865-1930), Pope Pius X's Secretary of State, lived from the age of two at Fulbeck (now Britannia Hotel) in Meyrick Road which belonged to his grandfather Don Pedro José de Zulueta, the Second Count de Torre Diaz, a former Speaker of the Spanish parliament. Raphael's father, the Marquis Raphael Merry del Val, was a diplomat at the Spanish Embassy in London and he and his wife Josephine also spent much time at the house. In 1871 Raphael and his elder brother had French lessons with four French nuns at The Lodge and then Mineham (later St Joseph's Convent since demolished) in Branksome Wood Road. This was the forerunner of the Convent of the Cross opened in 1887 in Boscombe (now Anglo European College of Chiropractic).

But his first school was St Aloysius (Premier Travel Lodge site) 8 Poole Road. The family attended, along with about 25 other Roman Catholics, the Sacred Heart Church which opened in 1870 as a wooden church and there Raphael had made his first communion in 1872. In 1875, just after the new church alongside had been opened, the family left for Brussels where his father was to be Ambassador. When the family lived at Fulbeck the hexagonal letterbox was newly placed on the north-west corner of the crossroads (now south-west) with five daily collections between 7 a.m. and 8 p.m.

MEWS, Sir Peter (1672-1727), MP for Christchurch, bought Hinton Admiral on the edge of the New Forest at the end of the 17th century. In 1708 he became Bournemouth's lord of the manor by buying, from the 2nd Earl of Clarendon, the Manor of Westover which was largely the parish of Holdenhurst embracing heath land destined to be central Bournemouth. The surname of his wife Lydia Jarvis (1676-1751) is the origin of the street name Gervis Place and 2nd baronet Sir George Tapps-Gervis* added the name having inherited Hinton Admiral.

MEYRICK, Sir George (1753-1835), 1st baronet. See George Tapps*.

MEYRICK, Sir George William (1795-1842), 2nd baronet. See Sir George Tapps-Gervis*.

MEYRICK, Sir George (1827-1896), 3rd baronet. See Sir George Tapps-Gervis-Meyrick*.

MEYRICK, Sir George (1855-1928), 4th baronet (Tapps-Gervis-Meyrick) and lord of manor. With his father, the 3rd Sir George Tapps-Gervis-Meyrick*, he agreed in 1883 to give Poors Common to the town. This was drained and the stream piped to create Meyrick Park. He also granted Bournemouth Corporation a lease for the Undercliff Drive from Bournemouth to Boscombe and sold Hengistbury Head to Selfridges' founder Gordon Selfridge who planned to build a castle on its highest point.

MEYRICK, Sir George Llewellyn (1885-1960), 5th baronet and lord of the manor who inherited in 1928, was Master of the New Forest Foxhounds. In 1935 Neville Chamberlain spoke at a Conservative fête held at his home Hinton Admiral.

MEYRICK, Sir George (1915-1988), 6th baronet, lord of the manor and soldier. In 1961, a year after succeeding to the title, he lifted the covenant imposed by the 3rd baronet preventing the Cat & Fiddle pub from opening on Sundays.

MILLS, 'Brusher' (1840-1905), snake catcher from 1885. His name came from his habit of sweeping or brushing cricket pitches in the New Forest where he lived in a hut and caught many adders without mishap. Lord Londesborough gave him a shilling for every snake caught and sent them to London zoo for use as food. Mills, a bearded figure with a stick, cleared the then swampy

Brusher Mills

Hinton Admiral, home of Sir Peter Mews and the Meyrick family

Queen's Park heath land of snakes before it became a golf course in 1905.

If there was a queue at the bar in his favourite Brockenhurst pub, the Railway Inn, he threw a couple of snakes on the floor to clear the way. He died at the inn and was buried in the churchyard in Brockenhurst where his stone is carved with snakes.

MILLS, Freddie (1919-1965), World Light Heavyweight Boxing Champion 1948, was born at 7 Terrace Road (since demolished) and attended St Michael's School in Somerville Road. He worked as a milkman and also a mechanic at the Majestic Garage (since closed) in Hinton Road and boxed at the Town Hall, Winter Gardens^, Dean Court football ground and 49 times at the Westover Ice Rink becoming British, Empire, European and World Light Heavyweight Champion. Alderman Frank McInnes kept a scrapbook of the fights for Freddie who used a room at the Brunswick Hotel in Malmesbury Park Road for training sessions. When living in Spring Road he drank at The Cricketers where after his death the function room became for several years the Freddie Mills Gymnasium. Mills was found shot dead in mysterious circumstances in an alley off London's Charing Cross Road. McInnes' son Peter, author of *Freddie My Friend* (Caestus Books), alleged that the Kray twins were involved in his death.

In 1979 an Italian marble memorial, designed by artist and fellow boxer Sam Rabin was placed in the gardens alongside Westover Road but following vandalism a replica was placed in the Littledown Leisure Centre. There is a blue plaque to him at St Michael's School entrance.

MONTGOMERY, Viscount (of Alamein) (1887-1976), Field Marshal met General Eisenhower at The Carlton Hotel for lunch in 1944 before watching from the cliff top a rehearsal for the Normandy D-Day landings. Lord Montgomery often returned to the hotel in peacetime. In 1969 he signed a copy of his book *A History of Warfare* whilst visiting the Town Hall.

MOODY, Richard (1813-1887), founder of British Columbia's capital New Westminster, died suddenly whilst staying at the Royal Bath Hotel and was buried in St Peter's churchyard near the Shelley tomb.

MOORE, Montague SS (1896-1966), VC, was born in Bournemouth and lived in Tower Road Branksome. His decoration was for capturing 28 Germans although his 70 men had been reduced to five near Ypres.

MOUNTBATTEN, Countess (Edwina) (1901-1960), wife of Lord Mountbatten*, often visited her great aunt Minna Cassel at Branksome Dene (now Zetland Court) in Alumhurst Road. In 1921 Edwina called to borrow a hundred pounds to follow Louis Mountbatten to India. She caught up with him at the Vice-Regal Lodge where he proposed. Shortly afterwards she inherited £6m from her grandfather Sir Ernest Cassel*.

MOUNTBATTEN, Earl (Louis) (of Burma) (1900-1979), Viceroy of India, laid the foundation stone of the War Memorial Homes in Castle Lane in 1946 on land donated by the Cooper-Dean estate. In 1973 he accepted an invitation from the Bournemouth Symphony Orchestra's guest conductor Sir Vivian Dunn, former Royal Marines Director of Music, to attend a concert at the Winter Gardens^. Lord Mountbatten was accompanied by his daughter Pamela Hicks and her husband David Hicks. A month later 'Lord Louis' became a life member of the Western Orchestral Society. In 1974 he attended a reunion of the Dorset & West Hants branch of the Burma Star Association at the Heathlands Hotel receiving a standing ovation and being sung out with *For he's a jolly good fellow*. In 1975 he was present at The Pavilion for a BSO fundraising concert conducted by Edward Heath* and Rudolph Schwarz*.

MOWLAM, Mo (Marjorie) (1949-2005), Labour cabinet minister, criticised the poll tax in 1988 when addressing the Fabian Society at the Friends Meeting House. Nine years later, on the eve of the 1997 victory Labour Party Conference, as Secretary of State for Northern Ireland, she recalled that meeting and of seeing her former history teacher Margaret Morley from a Coventry comprehensive school sitting in the front row. The teacher had inspired the girls to talk and argue claimed her former pupil. Miss Morley had subsequently become Headmistress of Avonbourne School.

In 1995 as the then shadow minister, Mo agreed to return and address the Bournemouth Labour Party at Lincoln Hall^ after appearing on BBC1's *Question Time* at the Littledown Centre. When Chancellor of the Duchy of Lancaster in May 2000 she opened the New Start project's 896 Club in Boscombe. Her last visit was a private one just before Christmas 2004 when she called on Miss Morley in Southbourne.

N

NASH, Eustace (1887-1969), artist, was born in Bournemouth and attended Drummond Road School of Art^. The weekly *Bournemouth Observer* was owned by his uncle Harry, proprietor of the Theatre Royal^. But Eustace became *Bournemouth Graphic's* cartoonist and continued to work in his first floor studio at 8 Albert Road studio after the newspaper had ceased publication. The *Observer* closed with the advent in 1900 of the *Bournemouth Daily Echo* which also had its office in Albert Road (now Bath Travel). The drawing of the present *Echo* office on the paper's masthead is probably the work of Nash. His drawings were familiar in promotional material commissioned by the Council. He worked in many media and travelled on trains and Hants & Dorset buses to produce Bournemouth and Poole travel posters as well as many watercolours.

Nash also exhibited in the Royal Academy of Arts summer exhibitions. In 1920 he was one of the founder members of the Bournemouth Arts Club and for many years supervised the club's life drawing evenings. He also ran his own in Albert Road where in 1940 the Arts Club started meeting as a wartime measure, which continued long into peacetime. Two of his watercolours of the new Pavilion were reproduced in the programme for its opening by the Duke of Gloucester* in 1929 and two years later he drew the cover picture of the programme for the opening of the Palace Court Theatre^.

He had lived at the family home Baernhurst 3 Talbot Road in Winton but that year he married and moved to Poole. He bought a house with £100 down payment received from the *Daily Mail* for designing the Christchurch village sign. He enjoyed playing the piano and joining Leslie Ward* in a boat to draw Poole Harbour scenes.

NASH, Paul (1889-1946), war artist, whose great uncle Canon Zachary Nash was curate and Vicar of Christchurch Priory Church from 1857 to 1883. In the 1930s Paul spent two years living in Swanage whilst writing the *Dorset Shell Guide* commissioned by John Betjeman*. During the Second World War he was a war artist (his work is now in the Imperial War Museum). He died in 1946 whilst staying at The Florida Hotel (Victory Court site) in Boscombe Spa Road. His last painting was the view across Boscombe Chine to the shelter above Honeycombe Chine.

NICOLSON, Nigel (1917-2004), politician and writer, was elected to Parliament as Conservative MP for Bournemouth East & Christchurch at a by-election on 6 February 1952. This was first day of Elizabeth II's reign and party officials at 30 Christchurch Road feared that electors would not turn out due to the unexpected announcement of George VI's death.

In 1956 Nicolson seconded the Death Penalty Suspension Bill and abstained in a Suez crisis vote of confidence. This brought local calls for his resignation and the Bournemouth East & Christchurch Conservative Association executive telegraphed the Prime Minister repudiating their MP. At the 1955 Conservative Party Conference at The Pavilion he attempted to speak on pensions but as he mounted the platform there was a cry of "Traitor! Traitor!" from the gallery and an intruder threw leaflets quoting him as saying that he did not consider Britain's membership of the UN inconsistent with his oath of loyalty to the Queen.

He also supported the recommendations on homosexual law reform proposed by the Wolfenden committee. The publication of *Lolita* by Weidenfeld & Nicolson, which he founded, brought him further opposition. In 1959 he lost a postal ballot of local Tory members by 3762 to 3671 and became the first Conservative MP to be deselected. The ballot has been described as Britain's first primary.

Towards the end of the century he said that opposing Suez was the best thing he had ever done. "Most people, even Conservatives, have come to agree that I was justified in what I did" he told Niam Attallah in an interview for *The Oldie* magazine. "And the fact that it meant the end of my political career added a note of semi-nobility to my action."

NOBLE, Cecil Reginald (1891-1915), VC, was born at 175 Capstone Road to a house painter Frederick and his wife Hannah. He attended St Clement's and St John's C of E School. In 1910 he joined the Rifle Brigade (Prince Consort's Own) and during the First World War he served in France. At the Battle of Neuve Chapelle he voluntarily rushed ahead and cut barbed wire impeding the advance of his battalion which was under machine gun fire. Corporal Noble died of his injuries and was posthumously awarded the VC. Noble Close in Wallisdown is named after him. The road is opposite Riggs Gardens which is named after fellow VC Charles Riggs* who also lived in Capstone Road.

NORFOLK, 14th Duke of (1815-1860), regularly stayed each summer at one of two 1849 villas which in 1870 were linked to form Stewart's Hotel on Richmond Hill. (Another villa next door survives as the Constitutional Club.) In 1910 the hotel was renamed the Norfolk Hotel.

The names of the 3 Bournemouth born holders of the Victoria Cross are commemorated on the statue outside the BIC

Stewart's Hotel, renamed Norfolk Hotel (subsequently the Norfolk Royale Hotel) after the Duke of Norfolk

The Duke found it handy for the Sacred Heart Church opposite. His brother Edward Fitzalan-Howard, the future 1st Baron Howard of Glossop, spent the winter of 1866-7 at Brunstath (The Carlton Hotel site) on the East Cliff where he had an oratory.

In 1988 the refurbished Norfolk Hotel was renamed the Norfolk Royale and opened by the 17th Duke who caused consternation by leaving an inkwell memento on the train home. Three months later it was returned by British Rail to the hotel where staff knew nothing of the loss although they had received a thank you letter from the Duke. After the present had been sent to the Duke's home he wrote expressing relief that the missing inkwell had been found.

Earlier the Duke had given permission for the Norfolk coat of arms, which had been on the front of the building since 1926, to remain. However, since the Duke was head of the College of Arms, the opportunity was taken during repainting to correct fifteen errors.

NORRIS, Philip (c1760-1806), early Boscombe resident who built 'Boscomb Cottage' which later became Shelley Park^. He probably inherited the land from his father Charles who was the owner in 1798. The edge of his estate to the west was Sea Road which he was responsible for keeping in good repair. Philip laid the foundation of the substantial estate later enjoyed by Sir Percy Shelley* by purchasing more land made available by auction under the 1802 Christchurch Enclosure Act. The 14 acres became more than 150 and on his death from a liver complaint were inherited by relative Richard Norris. After being briefly owned by Robert Heathcote until 1816, the now larger property was sold by auction at Covent Garden in 1817.

NORWOOD, Melita (Lettie) (1912-2005), longest serving spy in British history and most successful KGB spy allegedly enabling Soviet Union to develop a reactor and test an atomic bomb, was born in Pokesdown to an English mother Gertrude Stedman and a Latvian father Alexander Sirnis. He was a bookbinder who translated works by Lenin and Trotsky. The family was soon living with the Russian Tolstoyan community at Tuckton House (demolished in 1965) founded by Vladimir Tchertkov*. Her father died in 1918 and five years later Melita and her mother moved to Southampton.

O

ODLUM, Doris (1890-1985), leading child psychiatrist, Royal College of Psychiatrists founder fellow and MI5 agent, came from Folkestone to Bournemouth in 1898 with her parents who became the managers of the Metropole Hotel (site of Royal London House) at The Lansdowne. In 1901 she rode in a decorated carriage in a floral fete. She attended Bournemouth High School for Girls^ and in 1956, when it had become Talbot Heath School on its present site, she became a governor and later the chairman. On leaving school Doris was a suffragette campaigner and one of the first female Oxford graduates before embarking on a medical career.

In 1912 the family had bought the newly built Savoy Hotel and in 1922 Doris became chairman of the company on the death of her father. In 1928, at a time when the word 'psychiatry' was unknown, she set up at Boscombe Hospital one of the first general hospital departments of psychological medicine. She remained an honorary physician for psychiatry there until 1948. Although she held numerous appointments in London she later lived at Sandbanks and gave much time to the Bournemouth Samaritans' training sessions where she was known for her role playing. Before her death she endowed the BMA's Doris Odlum Prize for research work in psychiatry. The Doris Odlum Unit in Tower Road, home of the Bournemouth Adult Mental Health Psychology Team, is almost on the same site as her pioneer psychological medicine unit.

OGLE, Richard (1889-1976), artist who trained under John Singer Sargent and illustrated Enid Blyton's first book, *Boys Own Paper* and *Old Moore's Almanack*, lived at St Margaret's 18 Dingle Road from 1940.

OLD, Robert H (1878-1973), master tailor and founder of Robert Old & Co, studied economics alongside future dictator 'Benny' Mussolini before moving to Bournemouth in 1909 and opening a 'Tailors and Breeches Makers' at 189 Old Christchurch Road. The same year Old won the First Prize in the National Tailor & Cutter competition. Soon he moved to 5 Westover Road near today's location at number 21. For a time there were Robert Old & Co branches at Boscombe and Swanage.

In 1916 he had bought neighbouring Madame Campbell which was started by Annie Campbell but run by two German sisters who frightened customers. He opposed the building of The Pavilion but was an early supporter of The Square being traffic free.

In 1940 he was one of three councillors detailed to remain in the town if the Germans invaded. Maybe because his student friend had become a Hitler ally, Old was a strong believer in democracy being the best defence against dictatorship. He welcomed, as peacetime Mayor, the 1945 Labour Party Conference. The shop is now in the hands of his grandson Michael who was collected from the maternity home in the mayoral car.

ORTON, Joe (1933-1967), controversial playwright whose comic play *Loot* had its world première at The Pavilion in 1966. Around 20 people walked out of the theatre early in disgust. The following year he was murdered by his gay lover.

OSBORNE, John (1929-1994), award-winning playwright, was present in 1959 at The Pavilion for the world première of his play *The World of Paul Slickey*.

OSCAR II (1829-1907), King of Sweden & Norway, stayed at Crag Head (since rebuilt) in Manor Road during winter of 1881 with his wife Queen Sofia*. He laid the foundation stone of the Mont Dore hotel and 'bath establishment' (building is now Bournemouth Town Hall). The King and Queen became familiar figures with Bright's (now Dingles) and other shops granted the Swedish Royal warrant. In 1884 the Royal Yacht anchored in the bay. King Oscar, the last King of both Sweden and Norway, remains a familiar name in Sweden with King Oscar's Ginger Snaps on sale in shops.

Robert Old

Oscar II, King of Sweden with Queen Sofia

P

PAGE CROFT, Sir Henry (later Baron) (1881-1947), Conservative politician moved to Bournemouth having married Nancy Borwick, daughter of Lord Borwick in 1907. In 1910 they purchased The Knole^, former home of Edmund Christy*. In the same year Page Croft was elected MP for Christchurch, which included part of Bournemouth, having stood with the encouragement of Lord Malmesbury*. During the First World War, Page Croft fought at Ypres and the Somme. He remained MP until 1940 when he became a peer and Under Secretary for War in the Churchill* war coalition. The Knole^ was used by the army and as a nursery for evacuated London children. The Knole's front drive survives as Knole Gardens.

He was a friend of Sir Charles Cartwright*.

PALEY, Frederick Apthorp (1815-1888), leading Roman Catholic, classical scholar and writer, moved to Boscombe for his health in 1881. His home was Apthorp 2 Owls Road (since demolished) where he worked on the second edition of his commentary on the *Iliad.* Visitors included Friedrich von Hügel*. Part of Paley's library survives at Fitzwilliam College Cambridge.

PALMERSTON, 3rd Viscount (1784-1865), Prime Minister, visited the 3rd Earl of Malmesbury at Hurn Court. The 1st Lord Malmesbury had been Palmerston's guardian.

PARKER, Charles (1919-1980), radio producer, was born at 47 Richmond Park Road and attended Bournemouth School for Boys^. His disabled father sold paraffin from a barrow. The Centre for Broadcasting History Research holds an Annual Charles Parker Day Conference.

PARMOOR, 2nd Baron (1892-1977), nephew of Beatrice Webb* and eldest brother of Sir Stafford Cripps. After the Second World War he retired as Bursar of Queen's College Oxford and moved to Admirals Walk in Bournemouth where for his last four years the bachelor peer's household was run by a housekeeper.

PARRY, Sir (Charles) Hubert (1848-1918), composer whose work includes tunes for the Coronation anthem *I was glad, Jerusalem* and the hymn *Dear Lord and father of mankind.* His mother came to the town early in 1848 in advance of his birth which took place at the newly built 2 Richmond Terrace on Richmond Hill (site of number 16 below the surviving 4 Richmond Terrace). She died two weeks after the birth and was buried near the steps in St Peter's churchyard.

Two days later Parry was baptised by Morden Bennett* in the church before being taken to Gloucestershire. He returned in 1890 at the invitation of Dan Godfrey* to conduct the Bournemouth Municipal Orchestra in his English Symphony. Parry was a guest conductor for a Bournemouth Centenary Year concert of British music in 1910.

PEASE, Sir Joseph (1828-1903), Liberal MP and son of the first Quaker to sit in the House of Commons, lived at Ottershaw in Priory Road (now Bournemouth International Hotel) from about 1880, when it was built, until 1884. Stables faced the main road with the residence being in Beacon Road. In 1913 his son Joseph A Pease, President of the Board of Education, opened the Municipal College at The Lansdowne.

PETER II, King of Yugoslavia (1923-1970). The exiled King, fleeing his country after the German attack on Yugoslavia and accompanied by his prime minister, arrived at the Royal Bath Hotel in June 1941 to be welcomed to Britain on behalf of George VI by the Duke of Kent.

PLOWDEN, Alison (1931-2007), playwright, award-winning writer and prolific biographer of the Tudor and Stuart periods, was born in India but just before the outbreak of the Second World War moved to England with her mother who had separated from her husband. At her school she read historical novels which raised her interest in history and her ancestor Elizabethan lawyer Edmund Plowden. Her mother married Major-General H Lowry Davies (Taffy), official historian of the Far East Campaign, in 1948 and moved into his home 25 Meyrick Park Crescent. Later Alison left to work as a secretary at the BBC and whilst there decided to write having realised that she could produce better scripts than those she was typing.

POLLARD, Alfred Oliver (1893-1960), VC and author, was decorated for gallantry during an attack with only four men on German trenches in 1917. At the time the Second Lieutenant with the Honourable Artillery Company already held the MC and DCM.

In 1930 he published the first of over fifty thrillers and in 1949 moved to Bournemouth. At the time of his death he was living in a flat at 18 Queen's Park Gardens. His ashes are buried in Bournemouth North Cemetery.

PONTIN, Sir Fred (1906-2000), founder of Pontin's Holiday Camps which were said to have inspired the *Hi-Di-Hi!* television series, lived at The Penthouse at Pine Grange in Bath Road. His second wife was Joyce Hey who in 1962 had been recommended to him by his rival Sir Billy Butlin. She worked at his Bournemouth headquarters and gradually helped to oversee the expansion of Pontin's camps at home and in Europe. Pontin's was sold to Coral in 1978 and Fred and Joyce eventually married in 1999 by which time they had fulfilled their ambition to live in Blackpool.

PORTMAN, 1st Viscount (1799-1888), Liberal politician and relative of Lewis Tregonwell*. As a friend of Georgina Talbot* and he and his son William (2nd Viscount) were both among the original trustees of Talbot Village. In 1862 the first Lord Portman recommended Samuel Kerley as the first headmaster of Talbot Village School. From 1873, the year widower Baron Portman was raised to Viscount Portman, he was able to enjoy the same sea views as the Talbot household on the East Cliff when he built a holiday home called Wentworth Lodge (now Wentworth College) on the nearby Boscombe cliff top.

His main home was Bryanston near Blandford Forum and he had rented Portman Lodge* from his relative Henrietta, wife of Louis Tregonwell*. But over the next decade he spent about six weeks every summer at Boscombe. This seaside Italianate house, one of the earliest to be constructed of concrete, was erected by James Baker Green under the direction of concrete pioneer Charles Drake of the Patent Concrete Building Company. The garden frontage has a ground floor oval room with the Portman arms above. The grounds were protected from sea winds by a high bank on the south side and included a walled orchard, a kitchen garden and two seventy foot greenhouses.

The house was sold in 1923 on the death of the 2nd Viscount. The formal garden with its low tiled walls has been restored. The original carriage drive from the main road survives as Woodland Walk with its lodge now occupied by Deric Scott. Lascelles Road in Pokesdown recalls Lord Portman's wife Lady Emma Lascelles, daughter of the 2nd Earl of Harewood.

POTTER, Gillie (1887-1975), Oxford Bags inventor and actor famous for his monologues on the radio in the 1930s beginning "This is Gillie Potter speaking to you in English" from his fictional Hogsnorton, lived from 1962 with his

1st Viscount Portman

Portman Lodge, named after the Portman family

wife Beatrice in a flat at Gainslea Court Derby Road where he died. He attended St Stephen's Church whose director of music Percy Whitlock* wrote *Waltz: Revels in Hogsnorton* as the first movement of his *Wessex Suite* in 1937.

POWELL, Dilys (1901-1995), *The Sunday Times* film critic 1939-1976, was educated at Bournemouth High School^. She attended church and was confirmed but remained puzzled by religion for rest of her life whilst her school friend and fellow journalist Rosamund Essex* became an influential Anglican. In the early 1920s Dilys went abroad for first time when her father accompanied her to Southampton leaving her to cross to France alone in a single cabin. She returned with chickenpox.

In 1928 she arrived in London to seek a job in journalism after her father had given her £50 on the understanding that if she failed to secure work she would return to find a job as a teacher. *The Sunday Times* employed her to read proofs and to write a weekly leader that had to contain a little Latin. She is remembered by the Dilys Powell Award for Excellence in Cinema which has been won by Dirk Bogarde and Quentin Tarantino.

PRESTON, Kerrison (1884-1974), solicitor and art collector, was born in Boscombe, son of Donald Preston who had been a partner in Preston & Francis since 1876. He joined the firm in 1909 and in 1920 it became Preston & Redman.

He married his cousin Evelyn in 1912 and retired in 1949 to concentrate on his art collecting. Friends included George, father of Mary Spencer Watson*.

In 1953 Preston, a Blake scholar, published the edited letters of William Blake expert W Graham Robertson and in 1967, having moved to Merstham in Surrey, he presented his own Blake collection to Westminster City Libraries & Archives. St Julian's, his large house in Knyveton Road (since demolished for the building of Wimbledon Hall flats), was packed with pictures by Blake, GF Watts, Burne-Jones, Augustus John, Mark Gertler and Graham Sutherland. He also had a large library which included a first edition of Darwin's *The Origin of Species*, an original copy of TE Lawrence's *Seven Pillars of Wisdom* and an 1898 edition of *Chaucer's Complete Works* printed by the Kelmscott Press. He was chairman of the Bournemouth Arts Club which he addressed occasionally on old masters. He helped the Russell-Côtes Art Gallery to purchase Rossetti's *Venus Verticordia.*

PRICE, Robert (1905-1981), Dean of Hereford, was in 1942 invited by St Peter's Vicar Hedley Burrows* to be senior curate with responsibility for St Swithun's Church. When the vicar left the following year it was Price who took charge until the arrival of his successor Robert Boyd, Sir Thomas Beecham's brother-in-law. In 1945, two days after Price had accepted the living of Christchurch Priory Church, the vicar died and Price again took temporary charge of the parish. Twenty-two years later, having succeeded Burrows as Dean of Hereford and now retired, Price returned to St Swithun's Church to be priest-in-charge from 1968 to 1971.

PRICE, Stuart Hetley Price (1922-1977), Bishop of Ripon. His only curacy was at St Michael and All Angels Church in Poole Road from 1945 to 1948.

PRIESTLEY, JB (1894-1984), novelist and playwright, had lunch at the Royal Bath Hotel in June 1941 prior to writing an article for *Picture Post* which caused a storm. The author, who had a terrible experience fighting in the First World War, described the town as an escape from the war with comfortable hotels, opulent shops, thousands of well-dressed women, theatres, two orchestras, picture theatres and dinner dances. He suggested that as part of the war effort Bournemouthians should give up their accommodation to allow others to take a break.

The article was illustrated with pictures of Beales and other shops. "You can lounge at ease in quiet gardens and parks, where the azaleas and rhododendrons are flowering among the scented pines," he wrote and a picture, taken by Bill Brandt, showed him snoozing in the Royal Bath garden.

PUGIN, Peter Paul (1851-1904), church architect and the youngest son of Augustus Pugin, came to Bournemouth in poor health in December 1903. "When one gets weak, it takes time to pull up again," he wrote. His death in the town the following March is recorded on a plaque in the Pugin Chantry at St Augustine's Abbey in Ramsgate. His father Augustus, being a close childhood friend of Benjamin Ferrey*, had known Christchurch and buried his first wife in the Priory Church.

PUNSHON, William Morley (1821-1881), leading Methodist minister, spent Christmas and New Year in Bournemouth in both 1879 and 1880 to be with his sick thirty-year-old son John. He worshipped at the Church of the Holy Trinity^ on at least one occasion during the second Christmas visit as well as preaching at a Wesleyan Foreign Missionary Society service at the Town Hall (Top Shop site) in Old Christchurch Road. John died in January 1881 followed just two months later by his father.

In Canada Punshon had married his late wife's sister Mary who, as a widow again, moved to Bournemouth. Five years after his death the Punshon Memorial Methodist Church, a gothic building with a spire, was opened on the east side of Richmond Hill, just below Post Office Road. There were three churches in a row: the Church of the Sacred Heart (Roman Catholic), the Punshon and, at the bottom of the hill on the present NatWest site, St Andrew's Church (Scottish Presbyterian). The Punshon was built partly from the sale of The Tregonwell Arms (since demolished) and with help from a £10,000 Watering Places Chapel Fund raised years earlier by Dr Punshon for the erection of new churches in holiday resorts. A chancel window was dedicated to the memory of his son John.

The church was destroyed in 1943 by the wartime bombing raid which also devastated Beales and the Metropole Hotel. A replacement church, designed by Ronald Sims and awarded the RIBA bronze medal, was built in Exeter Road in 1958. After just 49 years this closed in 2007 due to falling attendances and serious structural problems. The last service was the Labour Party Conference Service when Prime Minister Gordon Brown read a lesson and Leslie Griffiths preached.

Sir Henry Page Croft

William Morley Punshon

R

RATTENBURY, Francis (1867-1935), architect. After designing several famous Canadian buildings, including British Columbia's Parliament and The Empress Hotel in Victoria, he returned to Britain in the early 1930s to live at Villa Madeira 5 Manor Road. He had met his young wife Alma at The Empress.

However, he was now bored, feeling old and drinking heavily. Meanwhile Alma, after advertising successfully in the *Echo* for a "Scout-trained" live-in handyman, fell in love with 18 year old George Stoner. He became jealous of the husband and clubbed Rattenbury who died four days later.

Alma took her own life by stabbing herself on the banks of the River Avon at Christchurch. A petition by many who blamed her for leading the young man on saved Stoner from the gallows. After eight years he was released from prison and lived in Bournemouth until 2000 dying on 24 March, the 65th anniversary of the murder.

Terence Rattigan* based his last play *Cause Célèbre* on the case. The television version starred Helen Mirren. Rattenbury was buried in Bournemouth Cemetery where a headstone, depicting the Canadian Parliamentary building, was erected in 2007. Mr and Mrs Rattenbury's son John moved to America where he became an architect.

RATTIGAN, Sir Terence (1911-1977), playwright, set his 1954 play *Separate Tables* in Bournemouth. He changed one page of the script to make the Major guilty of molesting women rather than importuning men on promenade to both avoid criticism from Lord Chamberlain and shocking his mother who attended all his first nights. The original script was discovered after his death and performed in 1998. His last play *Cause Célèbre* was based on the Rattenbury* case. At the time of his death two of his plays had just been performed at The Pavilion: *In Praise of Love* starring Richard Todd and *Flare Path*.

RAYMOND, Peter 'Teasy Weasy' Raymond Bessone (1911-1992), Britain's first celebrity hairdresser who invented the women's Page Boy style, introduced the open plan salon and employed the young Vidal Sassoon, opened Raymond

Art de Coiffure below Bourne Court in Bourne Avenue in October 1950 declaring that, "in future London and Bournemouth will set hair fashions." His other salons were in London and later in Cardiff. In 1963 he was the Liberal candidate in the South Kinson Ward coming second to Labour veteran George Spicer. Two years later Bournemouth resident Tony Standish was best man at his wedding to *Crossroads* actress Rosalie Ashley. The salon closed in 1969. Raymond was guest at the 1986 Mayor's fashion show.

REBBECK, William (1803-1879), founder of Rebbecks Estate Agent, lived in Ivy Cottage (Debenhams site) and was bailiff of the Tregonwell estate (east side of Exeter Road) under both Lewis Tregonwell* and his son John who eventually inherited following the death of his mother in 1846. He was also agent for the Drax estate which included Cliff Cottage (see Charles Darwin*) on the BIC^ site.

In 1840, when the church was a pair of cottages in The Square, he became St Peter's Church parish clerk at an annual salary of £5. In 1845 Rebbeck founded Rebbeck Brothers estate agents. The first office, designed by Decimus Burton*, was in The Square, on the corner of Old Christchurch Road and Gervis Place. (The building was demolished following a fire in 1885 and replaced but the site continued to be known as Rebbeck's Corner until 1935.)

Rebbeck lived next door at Gervis Villa and in 1872 he was chairman of the commissioners^. Rebbeck's funeral was the last for St Peter's vicar Morden Bennett* before his own death. Rebbeck is buried in the churchyard and is commemorated in the south window of the south-west transept. William's son Edward was Mayor of Bournemouth in 1892-3 and his grandson Col. Thomas Rebbeck was the 1936-7 Mayor. Since 1932 Rebbeck Brothers office has been on the far side of The Square.

REEVE, Henry (1813-1895), journalist and friend of Liszt and Thackeray, came to Bournemouth in April 1872 to visit his friend Lord Cairns* in Manor Road. At that time he rode out to Hengistbury Head and on the way saw the new village of Southbourne. A month later he returned and decided to build a house. Architect FP Cockerell was commissioned and work started in 1874 on Foxholes (Belle Vue Crescent) taking the name of the small copse below the high ground. Reeve lived there from April 1876 and spent much time enjoying the view of the sea, of Christchurch Harbour and the Highcliffe coast from his second floor loggias, while editing *The Edinburgh Review* and advising the publisher Longman.

Until 1887 he was Registrar to the Judicial Committee of the Privy Council but this only required occasional attendance in London. When he moved in he

William Rebbeck

Foxholes, Henry Reeve's home

had just been under attack for his publication of *Charles Greville's Memoirs* which were reported to have upset Queen Victoria as she was not forthcoming with an expected knighthood. He maintained a huge correspondence with leading figures at home and in Europe although Southbourne did not have its own Post Office until late in 1879.

During 1880s his wife Christine published *Manual of Domestic Economy* and provided an introduction to *Sermons for Children*. After his death at home, the house proved large enough in 1903 to become St Cuthbert's School, rented out for vegetarian holidays in August, and in 1937 a Workers' Travel Association guest house. In 1983 the building made way for 'Fox Holes' flats.

RENDALL, Athelstan (1871-1948), Liberal MP. Actively engaged as a politician between 1906 and 1924 and described as an Advanced Radical, he introduced the bill to allow a widow to marry her deceased husband's brother. Rendall lived in Branksome Park and was a partner in Rendall Litchfield & Co solicitors in Dean Park Road. In 1920 he founded, with three friends, Ferndown Golf Club.

RIGGS, Frederick Charles (1888-1918), VC, who in the First World War served in France, the Gallipoli campaign and Egypt, won the Military Medal during the Battle of the Somme. He was posthumously awarded the VC having died in action at Epinoy after capturing enemy guns and securing the surrender of fifty Germans.

His mother Ann was a cook and he lived at various addresses including 55 Garfield Avenue before settling at 39 Capstone Road (since demolished for building the Wessex Way) after being adopted by Elizabeth Burgum. He attended nearby Malmesbury Park School. On the outbreak of the First World War in August 1914 he was working for Pickford's removal firm. After a month he enlisted with the 15th The King's Hussars and the following year he was promoted to sergeant in the 6th Battalion, York and Lancaster Regiment whose museum at Rotherham now holds his medals. He is commemorated with plaques in his school and at 45 Capstone Road near his home. Riggs Gardens in Wallisdown is named after him. Cecil Noble* also lived in Capstone Road.

ROBERTS THOMSON, John (1844-1917), doctor and promoter of education and hospitals, came from Edinburgh in 1866 to take up an appointment at a cottage hospital in Madeira Road. Four years later he moved to the Royal National Hospital (now Brompton Court) in St Stephen's Road. He helped to establish the Royal Victoria Hospital (later the eye hospital) which opened in Westbourne in 1890. The following year he was President of the British Medical Association when the BMA Conference was held at the Theatre Royal^ in Albert Road which was then the temporary Town Hall. In his opening speech he called for every county to have a medical officer of health. He was a Liberal and among the first Bournemouth members of Hampshire County Council, when he represented the East Cliff Ward. He was a JP and as a supporter of the Volunteers rose to the rank of major in Hampshire Regiment.

His interest in education led him to become Chairman of the Drummond Road School of Art^, Science and Technology and help found Bournemouth School for Boys^ where he was the first chairman of governors. He was President of the Bournemouth YMCA and attended the Church of the Holy Trinity^ where in 1950, shortly after the death of his son William, the invalids' porch complete with fireplace was converted into the Roberts Thomson Memorial Chapel in memory of them both. He was made a freeman of the borough in 1913 and died at his home Monkchester (now part of Normandie Hotel) in Manor Road where he had a sea view from the back of the house.

ROBSON, Henry (1856-1932), grocer and first Scout camp quartermaster, arrived from Yorkshire in 1891 and took over a grocer's at the Triangle. The large long shop known as Robson & Son (public library site) had an arcaded pavement. He joined the Volunteer Fire Brigade and within six years he was a Liberal councillor.

In 1907 he helped Sir Robert Baden-Powell by nominating seven members of Winton Boys' Brigade to take part in the first Scout camp on Brownsea Island. Robson supplied the rations from his shop. On 29 July the Bournemouth boys, who did not know where they were going, were driven in a lorry by BB Captain Robson to Sandbanks where a Harvey's boat took them across to the island. There they met thirteen other boys, three from Poole, who were part of the ten day experimental camp. Baden-Powell described Robson as being "the greatest assistance to me in the preparation of our experimental camp".

One of the Winton boys was Terry Bonfield who became a carpenter and remained active in Scouting and at his death in 1991 he was able to say that he had met every Chief Scout. In 1909 Robson became a Vice-President of the new Bournemouth Scout Association. The following year Alderman Robson was on parade with the bands of the 1st Bournemouth and Wallisdown Companies when Baden-Powell addressed 174 scouts and scoutmasters at the Drill Hall (since converted into flats) in Holdenhurst Road.

During the First World War Robson was Mayor for two years from

Henry Robson

John Roberts Thomson

Charles Rolls

November 1915. Although he donated his mayoral allowance to the committee promoting tourism he was an early supporter of salaried councillors. He lived at Mulgrave 21 Meyrick Park Crescent.

Robson & Son and its branches, including one as far away as Swanage, closed in 1963.

ROE, Gordon (1932-1999), bishop, was born in Bournemouth and attended Bournemouth School^ where a fellow pupil was David English*. It was at school that he met his wife Mary during a play. From 1958 to 1961 he was curate at St Peter's Church where he assisted fellow curate Eric Evans* to found the Bournemouth Samaritans. Later Roe founded the Samaritans in Durham. In 1997, having been Bishop of Huntingdon, he retired to his wife's family house in Bournemouth.

ROLLS, Charles (1877-1910), aviator and Rolls-Royce co-founder. In 1910, two weeks after becoming the first person to fly the English Channel in both directions, he was Britain's first flying fatality when his biplane fell 20 feet at an air show on open ground, briefly known as Southbourne Aerodrome, between Southbourne and Hengistbury Head. The event was part of Bournemouth's centenary celebrations. Hangers were erected at the west end of Wick Lane on land now covered by the entrances to Brightlands and Broadlands Avenues but Rolls assembled his aircraft in a barn at Tuckton Farm (site of Peeks Mews between Iford and Riverside Lanes in Tuckton).

The night before he had dined with the show organiser Lady Abdy and told her: "I will fly with you this week but not in competition. Competition entails a certain amount of danger...there are more ways of flying than dying." His plane was taken to the field by van. Just before take off he signed an autograph for the driver's daughter and promised another to her friend when he returned. But, as he was circling to make a landing, the tail of his plane collapsed causing the aircraft to crash. He was first held in the arms of a local man who signalled to his 11 year old son George Morley, a St John Ambulance messenger, to bring water. Rolls died shortly afterwards in the arms of fellow aviator pioneer Sam Cody. A piece of the broken wooden propeller was given to the wife of the farm's foreman and later their son Bill Bartlett used the wood to make a model plane. A memorial marking the site of the accident was placed in the grounds of St Peter's School in 1978. Nearby is Rolls Drive which was the far end of the runway.

ROWE, Dorothy (1892-1988), co-founder of the Bournemouth Little Theatre Club and a friend of Dorothy L Sayers, attended Bournemouth High School^

from the age of four. After a period as an Oxford student she accepted a temporary teaching post at the school where she taught for forty years. In 1919 she helped to form the Bournemouth Dramatic and Orchestral Club which became the Little Theatre Club based for many years at the Palace Court Theatre^ and now in Jameson Road, Winton. She was passionate about Shakespeare and insisted in high standards in school and theatre.

RUSSELL-CÔTES, Sir Merton (1835-1921), art collector, traveller and Mayor who came to Bournemouth in 1876 due to ill health. On Christmas Day he bought the Bath Hotel and the following year met the Duke of Argyll in the hotel garden. He forecast that the hotel would be a goldmine. The Prince of Wales (Edward VII*) had stayed as a teenager so Russell-Côtes added the Royal prefix after refurbishing and extending the hotel. The dining room was based on the Egyptian Hall of London's Mansion House and in 1880 the Lord Mayor of London reopened the hotel whilst in the town to open the new pier.

The hotel was filled with Russell-Côtes' art collection; for a time he employed artist John Thomas to decorate the staircase walls. In 1881 the exiled Empress Eugenie* was amazed to see a piece of her own furniture in the collection.

Russell-Côtes pressed for the railway to be extended direct from Brockenhurst. This was achieved in 1888 after he had persuaded Sir George Meyrick* to allow the cutting across his land near Hinton Admiral.

Sir Merton also successfully lobbied for the proposed Undercliff Drive to be uncommercialised. He presented the mace to the new town council in 1890 and in 1894 he was elected Mayor without having first become a councillor although he had served as a commissioner^.

He greatly enjoyed welcoming notable guests including members of the Royal Family such as Prince Henry of Battenberg* and the Duchess of Albany.

Sir Henry Irving*, a friend, was a frequent visitor. His manager at the London's Lyceum Theatre, *Dracula* creator Bram Stoker, accompanied him on a visit to East Cliff Hall^ (now Russell-Côtes Art Gallery & Museum) to where Sir Merton and his wife Annie moved in 1901. They chose John Fogerty* as their architect but the final result is Sir Merton's idea of a fusion of 'Scottish baronial' and Italianate.

RUSTON, John (1933-1990), bookseller who had been encouraged to join the profession by EM Forster. In 1956, after working at Heffers in Cambridge, Ruston bought Horace G. Commin^ in Old Christchurch Road from Alan Thomas*. Ruston, known as JR to his friends, later claimed to be in awe of his customers who included Sir Kenneth Clark and Lord Montgomery*, Lawrence

Sir Merton Russell-Côtes

Durrell* and his brother Gerald Durrell* who featured the shop in his book *The Picnic and Suchlike Pandemonium.* Gerald often visited with a chimp from his zoo. Ruston's own shop companion was his Blue Point Siamese cat Marco. Ruston, who maintained and restored the mural on the shop stairs wall by Ian Fleming-Williams*, sold the shop in 1981.

RYAN, Vincent (1816-1888), Bishop of Mauritius. Following his return from Mauritius in 1867 he became Archdeacon of Suffolk. Two years later, deputising for the Bishop of Winchester, he consecrated the chancel and nave of the Church of the Holy Trinity^. In 1878 he preached there at a service to mark the completion of the tower. The church was an evangelical break-away from St Peter's Church so there was alarm when he was unexpectedly appointed to succeed Morden Bennett* at the mother church. Although Ryan respected the St Peter's tradition he was not popular with high church members whilst evangelicals were disappointed not to see changes. The following year, after just ten months, Bishop Ryan moved to the Ripon Diocese to help its bishop.

S

SCHWARZ, Rudolf (1905-1994), conductor. The Jewish Austrian musician was detained by the Germans in Belsen concentration camp but plucked from the queue for the gas chamber after an admirer requested a reprieve. In 1947 he was appointed conductor of the Bournemouth Symphony Orchestra. The Borough Treasurer Arthur Thatcher had mentioned to his son that, with the war over, the orchestra was going to appoint a conductor and he mentioned this to a school friend Kurt Schwarz who in turn told his uncle Rudolf.

Schwarz remoulded the orchestra before leaving in 1951 to be conductor of Birmingham Symphony Orchestra. In 1973 he returned as principal guest conductor and attended a lunch in his honour at the Highcliff Hotel. The two schoolboys AR Thatcher and Kurt Schwarz were among the guests. In 1975 he conducted the BSO at The Pavilion sharing the rostrum with Edward Heath*.

SCOTT, Elisabeth Whitworth (1898-1972), great-niece of Sir George Gilbert Scott, feminist and first woman architect to win a major architectural competition, was born at Hartington in Poole Road, a house where Cardinal Merry del Val* had been to school and Verlaine* had taught. Her father was Dr Bernard Scott (founder of the practice which became the Westbourne Medical Centre) and brother of Dr Thomas Bodley Scott*). Her mother was the daughter of architect GF Bodley. The family lived next door to her uncle at Chadwell House 119 Poole Road where she was taught until the age of fourteen when she attended school in Canford Cliffs.

Elisabeth exhibited her paintings locally. After briefly being secretary to a Labour MP she enrolled in 1919 with the Architectural Association Schools. In 1928 she won the competition to design the Shakespeare Memorial Theatre at Stratford-upon-Avon. Her proposal noted for its brickwork was commended by George Bernard Shaw as the only one that showed any theatre sense. She later worked with Ronald Phillips & Partners and in 1962, as Mrs George Richards, joined Bournemouth Council architects department where her projects included the Bournemouth Pier theatre and café and the pavilion on Boscombe Pier.

SCOTT, George Henry Robert (1880-1948), founder of undertakers George Scott & Son, was the grandson of George Henry Scott who is said to have brought the first steam roller to the town. Third generation George opened his cabinet maker and funeral business in Boscombe's Somerset Road in 1899. The business became established enough to be awarded the contract for the many military funerals during the First World War. Directors in 2010 include his great grandson Neil.

SCOTT, John (1854-1924), Mayor and grandfather of Deric Scott, was an apprentice carpenter to George Lawson*. In 1884 John founded John Scott & Sons at 121 Haviland Road. In 1910 he moved to Spurgeon Road allowing his son Ernest to move into the family home for the birth of grandson Deric (1910-1997). He eventually bought the business, then known as Ernest J Scott Ltd, and in addition to making windows, staircases and coffins he offered funeral services. By 1940 he was concentrating on funerals under the name Deric S Scott. The business moved to Wentworth's Lodge in 1966.

SCOTT, Nick (1933-2005), Conservative MP and minister, was arrested during the 1996 Conservative Party Conference on being found collapsed in a gutter one evening after attending an Irish Embassy reception. Alcohol had reacted with painkillers taken for a back condition but his Kensington constituency party was unsympathetic and he was deselected prior to the General Election the following year.

SEAGRIM, Derek Anthony (1903-1943), VC, was born at 14 Charminster Road whilst his father Charles Seagrim was briefly curate at St Peter's Church. He died two weeks after leading a night attack during the Second World War on a German line in Tunisia for which he was decorated.

SECOMBE, Sir Harry (1921-2001) entertainer and singer. Commenting on St Peter's Church during a *Songs of Praise* filming he said: "This must be one of the most beautiful churches in the country I have seen." In 1995 during 'A Weekend Called Fred' conference at the Manchester Hotel he gave a long interview about The Goon Show.

SELFRIDGE, Gordon (1858-1947), founder of Selfridge's department store in London, bought all the land east of Southbourne from Sir George Meyrick* in 1919. At the time he was renting Highcliffe Castle as a country home and planned to build a castle for himself on Hengistbury Head. He described it as "the biggest house in the world" and commissioned plans from architect Philip

Tilden. In 1930 Bournemouth Corporation bought the land to preserve the natural coastal feature.

SERGEANT, Adeline (1851-1904), prolific novelist, life-long contributor to *The People's Friend* and an early Fabian. In 1901 she moved from London to Agincourt House in Albert Road. This was handy for the Church of the Sacred Heart which she attended, having converted to Roman Catholicism in 1899 and written about her decision in *Roads to Rome, being Personal Records of Some of the More Recent Converts to the Catholic Faith*. Fellow author Ellen Thorneycroft Fowler* and the widow of William Morley Punshon* were among her friends. She died at the Tollard Royal Hotel (now the Tollard Court) next to the Highcliff Hotel.

SHACKLETON, Edward (Baron) (1911-1994). Cabinet minister and son of Sir Ernest Shackleton* who had given his South Pole lecture at the Winter Gardens^ in 1910. In the 1945 Bournemouth by-election, caused by Sir Leonard Lyle's resignation, Shackleton stood as the Labour candidate. His slogan was 'With Shackleton to the poll'. He borrowed a car from party member Bertha Middleton to get around the constituency canvassing but lost to Brendan Bracken*.

SHARP, Graham (1917-1995), champion ice skater. He started when aged twelve skating at the Westover Ice Rink which had just been opened in Westover Road by his father. In 1938 he was captain of the British Olympic figure team at Garmisch-Partenkirchen and in 1939 won the world skating title at Budapest. His hopes for the 1940 Olympics were dashed by the Second World War when he served in the army. In 1948 he carried the Union Jack at the Winter Olympics held at St Moritz. His final performance was in 1948 when his father died and Graham had to succeed him as managing director of the ice rink and adjoining Westover Garage. He left the town in 1974.

SHELLEY, Jane (Lady) (1820-1899), wife of Sir Percy Shelley*, was largely responsible for assembling and maintaining the PB Shelley relics at Shelley Park^ and defending his reputation. She did not feel that the biography written by Shelley's student friend Thomas Jefferson Hogg was effusive enough although he had been briefed by her at Boscombe. Richard Garnett, Keeper of Printed Books at the British Museum, and his wife Jane often visited but he declined the offer of being Shelley's official biographer although he had written extensively about him and published *Relics of Shelley* in 1862.

In 1861 Jane had hosted a table at the Belle Vue Hotel during the dinner

Gordon Selfridge

Sir Percy Shelley

celebrating the opening of Bournemouth Pier. In 1888 she 'drove' the first pile for Boscombe Pier which opened the following year. She was instrumental in her family giving the land in 1891 for St Andrew's Church in Florence Road which was a tin building until the present structure opened in 1907. She bequeathed Boscombe Cliff Gardens to the town.

SHELLEY, Mary (1797-1851), author of *Frankenstein* and wife of PB Shelley*, probably never visited the 19th-century Boscombe Manor (now Shelley Park^) which her son Percy Florence Shelley* bought with the intention of Mary living there. She died at home in London before the move could be arranged and is buried in St Peter's churchyard along with the remains of her parents William Godwin* and Mary Wollstonecraft* which were removed from the London churchyard at St Pancras in 1851 to make way for the railway.

SHELLEY, Percy B (1792-1822), poet and leading figure in the Romantic Movement. His heart, snatched from his cremation fire on Viareggio beach in Italy, is buried in the family tomb in St Peter's churchyard after being kept by his son Sir Percy Shelley* at Boscombe. The poet never visited the area but may have known of it from his cousin and first serious girlfriend Harriet Grove who lived in Dorset and with whom he kept up a regular correspondence. He sent her personal poems. During the courtship she stayed at Mudeford and was taken to 'Bourn' by Lewis Tregonwell* and his wife on Wednesday 4 July 1810 to see where their house was to be built. Harriet's verdict was "very barren but a pretty sea view".

SHELLEY, Sir Percy Florence (1819-1899), son of poet Percy B Shelley*. He purchased Boscombe Manor (now Shelley Park^) in 1849 for his mother Mary Shelley* rather than himself but after she died in 1851 it was enlarged to become the principal residence of Sir Percy and his wife Jane*. The original house was built in 1801 as Boscombe Cottage. The garden had mulberry trees and included the cliff inlet Honeycombe Chine, soon known as Shelley Chine.

Apart from the initial building work, when Shelley stayed at the (Royal) Bath Hotel, he later agreed to more changes and eventually the house had fifteen bedrooms and stables for six horses. The cliff top grounds stretched from Sea Road at the side of Boscombe Chine to today's Browning Avenue.

Behind a curtain in the house was an alcove where Shelley's heart was kept in a vase. A red lamp was always burning in front and surrounding it were numerous documents which now form the Shelley collection at Oxford's Bodleian Library. Also in the house were portraits of both Mary Wollstonecraft* by John Opie and PB Shelley* by Amelia Curran which have

SOFIA (1836-1913), Queen of Sweden & Norway, stayed at Crag Head (rebuilt as flats) on the cliff-top in Manor Road with King Oscar* in 1881. One of her first public appearances was for Sunday afternoon evensong at St Peter's Church. Visitors at Crag Head included Empress Elizabeth* and Empress Eugenie*. Sofia returned to Crag Head in 1888 for two months and was present at the wedding of her son Prince Bernadotte* at St Stephen's Church. Crag Head had stained glass depicting the Swedish Royal arms.

SOMERSET, Nina (1893-1983), artist, moved during the Second World War to 451 Charminster Road where she had a seemingly chaotic studio. She attended Mass daily at nearby St Francis of Assisi Church; her work included the crucifix and lampshades in the Blessed Sacrament Chapel and a banner. She was responsible for the Stations of the Cross at St Stephen's Church and a banner for St Alban's Church, Charminster. She also produced Christmas and Easter posters. Much of her work can be seen at St Silas Church in London's Kentish Town where she attended in the 1920s.

SOUTHAMPTON, 2nd Earl of (1545-1581), father of Shakespeare's patron, wrote in 1574: "wee find at Burnmouthe, a place verry easy for the ennemye tolande, there conteyning by estimacion over aquarter of a myle in length, being voyde of all inhabiting."

SOUTHEY, Robert (1774-1843), Poet Laureate, was accompanied by his wife Edith when in June 1797 he rented a cottage at Burton near Christchurch. He had just been granted an annuity which bought time to write. Within a few weeks he visited Lady Strathmore* at Stourfield House which he described as "finely situated". Southey was impressed by the Spanish and Italian spoken by the Countess who bombarded him with invitations to visit. Although irritated by her demands he enjoyed having access to her library. He described walking east across Poole Heath, soon to become Bournemouth, as "walking through desolation". Just before leaving Burton in mid September he also walked along the beach from Southbourne to Sandbanks in order to reach Corfe Castle but was prevented by bad weather from crossing at the Poole Harbour entrance.

SPELLER, Cyril (1919-1990), Bournemouth Fabian Society Secretary, who unmasked Major James Friend as a member of the Empire Loyalists. Friend had been selected as Conservative candidate to succeed the deselected Nigel Nicolson*. Speller was a friend of Bob Edwards, editor of *Tribune*, who used to visit the town weekly to check proofs before the paper was printed on the *Bournemouth Times* presses. The following morning he usually joined Speller for breakfast on the train to London. With such contacts Speller was well-placed to expose a local politician caught up in a national crisis. When Nicolson was showered with hostile leaflets it was Cyril Speller who recognised key phrases as being identical to a letter published under Friend's name in the *Bournemouth Daily Echo*. He denied being an Empire Loyalist but subsequent revelations by Speller resulted in the resignation of Friend. Speller was Labour agent during the 1959 General Election and at the count he was able to tell winner John Cordle that he was the MP thanks to the action of a Labour supporter.

SPENCER WATSON, Mary (1913-2006), sculptor, who lived and worked for 83 years at Dunshay Manor near Corfe Castle. In 1923 when her parents went to view the house they discovered Lucy Kemp-Welch* staying there on a holiday. In 1928, at the age of 15, Mary travelled once a week to Bournemouth School of Art^ where she made a relief in Portland stone of the Elgin Marbles horse's head – a forerunner of her much later work.

Having been trained by her father George Spencer Watson RA, she was ahead of other students and in 1930 went on to the Slade School of Art. That year she attended the opening of the Gallery Studio, the Bournemouth Arts Club's new home at 45 Poole Hill. In 1931 her father exhibited with the Club and in 1935 became its President. Towards the end of the decade Mary got to know Paul Nash* who was living in Swanage.

SPRAGUE, Ken (1927-2004), artist, graphic designer, stage designer and newspaper cartoonist, was born in Bournemouth on New Year's Day. His father was an engine driver and his mother worked in a cardboard box factory. He was brought up in Winton and attended Alma Road School and Porchester School from where he won a scholarship at the age of 13 to the Bournemouth College of Art^. At the age of ten he had already made a lino cut about the bombing of Guernica which was used by supporters of the anti-fascist forces in Spanish Civil War. After wartime service as a Royal Marine and technical artist, he returned to complete his art course.

STEVENSON, Robert Louis (1850-1894), author, stayed at the Highcliffe Hotel in July 1884 whilst looking for a house. (The hotel had yet to drop the 'e' from its name to avoid confusion with Highcliffe near Christchurch.) After a week he and his wife Fanny moved to the cheaper Sunnington Rise guest house in West Cliff Gardens. In November after several more moves they rented a house in Branksome's Burton Road.

This was near their eventual home Sea View (bombed in 1940) in Alum Chine Road which was a wedding present from his father. From April 1885 to

Robert Southey

Robert Louis Stevenson

Ken Sprague

August 1887 they lived there with Fanny's 16 year old son Lloyd Osbourne who was already attending Saugeen School^. Fanny renamed the house Skerryvore^ after a lighthouse built by Robert's uncle and extended the garden down into Alum Chine. She enjoyed the apple trees and grew tomatoes. "The drawing room is a place so beautiful that it is like eating to sit down in it" Stevenson wrote. At the house he finished *Kidnapped* and, after a dream, he wrote *The Strange Case of Dr Jekyll and Mr Hyde* where the butler is given the name Poole.

American artist JW Alexander called to draw Stevenson's head and John Singer Sargent came to paint him standing in the drawing room. Sargent told Henry James*, who had a special chair for his visits, that Stevenson "seemed…the most intense creature I have ever met". Other visitors included Lady Taylor (wife of Sir Henry*) and his doctor Thomas Bodley Scott* who had to deal with his lung haemorrhage, influenza and frequent depression.

Stevenson claimed to live at his house like "a weevil in a biscuit" but when well enough on Sundays he attended St Peter's Church. Often a haemorrhage attack would cause him to leave the church early and walk to Blacklock's^ chemist in The Square where pharmacist Frank Spinney looked after him until friends from church drove him home.

He managed a visit to Dorchester to meet Thomas Hardy* but found a local trip to Sir Henry Taylor* at The Roost easier. His daughter Una helped with music composition. With Fanny he attended theatrical evenings at Shelley Park^. Two years after leaving the town in 1887 he dedicated his next novel *The Master of Ballantrae*, published in 1889, to Sir Percy and Lady Jane Shelley*. In the year of his departure he published his collection of poems *Underwoods*.

The couple continued to write to a young girl called Adelaide Boodle who lived in Poole Road and had received writing lessons from the author. The day he left Bournemouth he suddenly realised how much he loved the area and the house where he was looked after by a housekeeper and a maid.

STONEHOUSE, John (1925-1988), MP and confidence trickster who went missing in mysterious circumstances. In 1939, as pupil of evacuated Taunton's School in Southampton, he arrived in Bournemouth to attend Bournemouth School. He walked daily to the school from his accommodation chatting about politics to a junior boy Stan Holmes. As Postmaster General, Stonehouse returned to the town to address the Socialist Ladies Luncheon Club at the Wessex Hotel.

STRATHMORE, Countess of (Mary Eleanor) (1749-1800), colliery millionaire's daughter who was the inspiration for William Thackeray's novel *The Luck of Barry Lyndon*, married John Lyon who became the 9th Earl of Strathmore. In 1795 the widowed Countess moved to Stourfield House in Southbourne (Douglas Mews site where the sweeping double outside staircase survives). The mansion, built about 1766, had a greenhouse, dovecote and ice house. The grounds stretched down the hill as far as Cranleigh Road. She moved to this then remote Georgian house, with a view of St Catherine's Hill and Christchurch Priory Church, to avoid her impecunious second husband Captain Andrew Stoney (of 'Stoney broke' fame) who had kidnapped her in London in an Oxford Street shop and held her hostage in a castle near Newcastle.

At Stourfield visitors included future Poet Laureate Robert Southey* who walked over from Burton and enjoyed browsing in her library. He considered that to go any further west he would be "walking through desolation". Her young adult children Lady Anna Jessop (who had impulsively married secretly at Gretna Green) and Mary (from second marriage) lived with her. A maid Mary Morgan, who had helped her escape from the castle, died in 1796 and was buried in Christchurch Priory Church. A footman Robert Crundall, once sacked by Stoney for giving evidence against him, was in attendance. Food and beer was often sent to the Tuckton farmhands in the fields below. The countess had many dogs and a great interest in plants.

Following her death at the house in 1800 she was clothed in her wedding dress from her first wedding prior to burial in Westminster Abbey. Her maiden name 'Bowes' was added to the Earl's family name which became Bowes-Lyon and as a result the arms of her great great granddaughter Queen Elizabeth, The Queen Mother* included bows.

STREET, George Edmund (1824-1881), architect. His commissions in Bourne-mouth were at the invitation of Morden Bennett*, the first vicar of St Peter's Church. In 1853 Street had been invited to rebuild St Peter's but first Bennett asked him to design a small church for Moordown. This, the original St John's Church, was completed in 1854 and extended eastwards eleven years later. (The building, on the east side of Wimborne Road just south of Malvern Road, is in residential use.) By the end of the decade Street had presented designs for the new church of St James and its school at Pokesdown. The new St Peter's Church was opened on Christmas Day 1859. In 1865 St Barnabas Church at East Parley (since closed), a mission church designed by Street and served from St Peter's Church, was completed. The following year he was working on plans for his most famous building, the Royal Courts of Justice.

Around this time he also designed the first St Michael's Church which was demolished when the present building by Street's pupil Norman Shaw was built. It was not until December 1879 that a service of thanksgiving was held for the completion of St Peter's Church. Bennett died a month later.

SULIVAN, Sir Bartholomew James (1810-1890), admiral who sailed with Charles Darwin* on The Beagle and father of Falkland Sulivan, the first British subject born in the Falkland Islands. In 1865 Sulivan moved to Bournemouth to live at Tregew (25 and 27 bungalows site) in Gervis Road named after the place of his birth Tregew in Cornwall. His friend Richard Potter asked the retired naval officer to look after his daughter Beatrice (Webb*) who was at boarding school at the end of the road. On Sundays he took Beatrice to Holy Trinity Church^. The Admiralty was consulting him as late as 1878 and he remained a life-long friend of Darwin*.

SUMNER, Heywood (1853-1940), arts and crafts artist, archaeologist and friend of William Morris. In 1893 Sumner and his wife Agnes moved from London to live at Skerryvore^ in Westbourne, the former home of Robert Louis Stevenson*. Their son Benedict, historian and Warden of All Souls Oxford, had just been born. During the next few years his father was busy with sgraffito designs for All Saints Church, Ennismore Gardens in London (now a Russian cathedral) and St Agatha's Church Portsmouth and work in Essex and Oxfordshire.

He described Bournemouth as a garden city because it had "miles and miles of houses in gardens". He took long bicycle rides around the New Forest which he loved and in 1883 illustrated *The New Forest* by John R Wise. With his wife in poor health he decided to buy land there to design and build his famous Cuckoo Hill house which by 1904 became the home of the couple and their five children. Over the next twenty years he spent much time on archaeological surveys and in 1921 the Bournemouth Natural Science Society published one of his reports called *Ancient Earthworks of the Bournemouth District.*

SWINBURNE, Algernon Charles (1837-1909), poet, in January 1863 visited his sick sister Edith who was taken seriously ill and expected to die. She recovered enough to be taken back to his home at East Dene on the Isle of Wight where she died in September. He was much affected by this traumatic year which may have had an effect on some chapters of his novel *Lesbia Brandon.*

SYDENHAM, John (1782-c1860), publisher of the first Bournemouth guide book, was a bookseller from Poole who in 1840 opened a stationery shop with reading room and library next to the Belle Vue Hotel opposite the future pier. The Bourne Stream ran along the western side from the meadows behind. The reading room with plenty of newspapers and magazines as well as refreshments was a popular meeting place. Visitors often called in to collect mail delivered to the 'receiving box'. Sydenham had produced *The Visitors Guide to Bournemouth* in 1840.

Later guides were the work of the family including his Poole-born wife Elizabeth and daughter Anne. His great nephew Reginald set up Sydenham's Printing Works in Oxford Road producing Sydenham's postcards. Third son David pioneered steamer trips from the Pier. In 1865 the library moved across the road to a new building at the foot of the East Cliff (IMAX site) where in 1877 it was renamed as the Royal Marine Library. The building, with bay windows and a turret, was demolished in 1934 to make way for the Pier Approach Baths.

John Sydenham's Reading Room, next to the Belle Vue Hotel

T

TALBOT, Sir George, 3rd Baronet of Mickleham, Surrey and of Belfast, County Antrim (1763-1850). He was the father of Georgina Talbot* and Mary Anne Talbot* and descendant of John Talbot mentioned in Shakespeare's *Henry VI Part 1.* The widowed Sir George Talbot moved with his daughters from Mickleham to Bournemouth in 1849 where he bought Hinton Wood House (since rebuilt as flats) on the East Cliff.

TALBOT, Georgina Charlotte (1793-1870), co-founder of Talbot Village, moved with her father Sir George Talbot* and sister Mary Anne* to Hinton Wood House (site now flats) in East Overcliff Drive. Living in a comfortable house with Chippendale chairs, the two women were much moved by the plight of the poor from the countryside who drifted into the town seeking work. Inspired by a German book called *The Goldmaker's Village*, Georgina developed the idea, with the support of her sister, of a model village. After inheriting Portobello Farm in London's Portobello Road in 1850 they decided to sell the Notting Hill property and raise £150,000 to buy land just over the Hampshire boundary and build a village. The 16 cottages resemble those in Mickleham in Surrey where the sisters were joint patrons of the church. Each cottage had a pigsty and fruit trees land was let at a fair rent. Georgina purchased the bellcote from Bournemouth's first church (the forerunner of St Peter's Church on Debenhams site) for the school designed by Christopher Crabbe Creeke*. There were also five farms. Georgina's funeral was the first to take place in the church and her burial was the first in the churchyard.

The sisters' other legacy was Winton which was named after their relative the Earl of Eglinton & Winton whose title is derived from Winton House outside Edinburgh. Winton Banks parade of shops was originally known as Talbot Park and The Talbot Hotel, complete with coat of arms, is on the corner of Wimborne Road and Pine Road.

Georgina also had a house in London's Grosvenor Square.

TALBOT, Mary Anne (1788-1885), co-founder of Talbot Village, eagerly joined her sister Georgina Talbot* in creating Talbot Village and continued the project after her younger sister's death in 1870 by adding three more cottages including one for the church organist. GF Watts painted her in the year she died.

TAPPS, Sir George (1753-1835), 1st baronet and lord of the manor, inherited Hinton Admiral in 1778 from his cousin William Clerk. (Later the family name was called Meyrick.) He began planting his land with pines before the turn of the century and added more after the 1803 Christchurch Enclosure Award gave him the gorse covered heath land at Bourne Mouth. The owner of Stourfield, Edmund Bott who preceded the Countess of Strathmore*, also planted pines prior to 1795.

The Tapps Arms, used by fisherman and now the site of Post Office Road entrance in Old Christchurch Road, opened in 1809. Tapps sold a plot of land to Lewis Tregonwell* in 1810. In 1829 Tapps gave a piece of land in Holdenhurst for the present church to replace the Saxon church which stood a hundred yards away. This was in a bad state of repair and the builder was allowed to demolish it and dispose of the materials despite an earlier plan to incorporate them in the new building.

TAPPS-GERVIS (Meyrick), Sir George William (1795-1842), 2nd baronet, lord of the manor. He was MP for Christchurch, which included Bournemouth and was the son of Sir George Tapps*. The young Sir George, on succeeding the baronetcy in 1835, assumed the additional name of his distant relatives Gervis. (The wife of his ancestor Sir Peter Mews* who had lived at Hinton Admiral in the 18th century was Lydia Jarvis.) He employed Benjamin Ferrey* as architect to lay out a marine village along the east side of the River Bourne. This included Westover Road and on Queen Victoria's Coronation Day in 1838 he opened the (Royal) Bath Hotel. In 1841 he paid for work to start in September on St Peter's Church. His wife was Clara Fuller through whom the name Meyrick was later adopted. His early death in 1842 saw his heir succeed as a minor.

TAPPS-GERVIS-MEYRICK, Sir George (1827-1896), 3rd baronet and lord of the manor who succeeded the baronetcy in 1842 at the young age of 15. He assumed from his grandfather the name and arms of Meyrick in 1876 by Royal licence; later generations adopted the simple single surname of Meyrick.

He employed Decimus Burton* to enhance the plans for developing Bournemouth but he was extremely reluctant to allow the railway to be built across his land to create the direct link from Southampton to Bournemouth. He was eventually persuaded by his wife Fanny and Merton Russell-Côtes* and in return a convenient station, Hinton Admiral, was built in 1886 ahead of the line opening in 1888. However, the drunken behaviour of Irish labourers laying the lines led him to impose a restricted covenant on The Cat & Fiddle pub preventing it from opening on Sundays. The ban remained until 1961. He presented Meyrick Park to the town.

TAPPS-GERVIS-MEYRICK, Sir George (1855-1928).
See Sir George Meyrick; 4th baronet.

TAPPS-GERVIS-MEYRICK, Sir George (1885-1960).
See Sir George Meyrick; 5th baronet.

TAPPS-GERVIS-MEYRICK, Sir George (1915-1988).
See Sir George Meyrick; 6th baronet.

TAYLOR, Eleanor (1847-1911), writer, was daughter of Sir Henry Taylor*. In 1872 her novel *Alcestis* was published anonymously but admired by Tennyson. Later she lived in Boscombe when she was the wife of Charles Seymour Towle, vicar of St Clement's Church from 1892 to 1908. During this time she became friendly with Aubrey Beardsley*. The font cover at St Clement's Church is a memorial to her and was dedicated in 1912 by Father EF Russell of St Alban's Church in Holborn, London who had edited her biography of its famous vicar Alexander Mackonochie. She is buried with her husband outside the east end of St Clement's Church.

TAYLOR, Harry (1911-1999), photographer, was born in London and moved to the Bournemouth area in 1939 to work in a Poole shipyard. After the war he set up a photographic studio and during the 1950s and 1960s photographed many celebrities visiting Bournemouth. He most famous pictures were of the Beatles* in 1964 and 1965 and included the four eating rock whilst standing on a balcony at the Palace Court Hotel^ (now Premier Lodge) in Westover Road. His Beatles collection, 38 negatives and 21 prints, was sold at Christie's in 2008 for over £9,000.

TAYLOR, Sir Henry (1800-1886), author, poet and friend of Tennyson and Robert Southey*. On a visit to Bournemouth in May 1861 Taylor wrote: "The place is beautiful beyond any seaside place I have ever seen except the Riviera." In the poem *St Clement's Eve* composed at the time he noted the "pine groves" and then still plentiful "honey-scented heather". His holiday home, The Roost (since demolished) 17 Hinton Road, was built the following year. His many visitors included Sir Percy Shelley* who first met Robert Louis Stevenson*

Count Vladimir Tchertkov's printing press at Tuckton

there, Lady Taylor's cousin the Irish poet Aubrey de Vere, Bacon's biographer James Spedding and Auberon Herbert.

As an admirer of Mary (Wollstonecraft*) and William Godwin*, Taylor was interested to find the couple buried in the nearby St Peter's churchyard. In 1869 Lord John Russell promoted a Life Peerage Bill with a view to Taylor being one of the recipients but it was defeated in Lords due to a speech by the 3rd Lord Malmesbury*. Taylor retired from the Colonial Office in 1872 and became a familiar figure with his beard and flowing white hair. He died at The Roost and was buried behind the chapel of rest in nearby St Peter's churchyard.

TAYLOR, Una (c1854-1922), author, who as the youngest daughter of Sir Henry Taylor*, was well placed to write *Guests and Memories* (1925) recording life at her father's house in Hinton Road. In 1884 she worked as a librettist with Hubert Parry* on his *King Arthur's Farewell to Guenever* and helped Robert Louis Stevenson* with musical composition. During her life she was a frequent contributor to *The Edinburgh Review*. In 1887 her novel *The City of Sarras* was published, followed on 1896 by *Nets for the Wind* in John Lane's *Keynote Series* which had a cover in the style of Aubrey Beardsley* who had designed the original series covers. Strangely by that year he was living at Boscombe and a friend of her sister Eleanor Taylor*. Una also wrote *Maurice Maeterlinck: a critical study* which was published in 1914. She was also good at embroidery and shared a home near New Milton with her sister Ida.

TCHERTKOV, Count Vladimir (1854-1936), was deported from Russia in 1897 for his progressive views and the following year moved into Tuckton House (demolished in 1965) in Saxonbury Road Tuckton near his mother Elizabeth Tchertkov*. He formed a community and in 1898 set up a printing press at the riverside Old Waterworks in Iford Lane. There until 1913 the Free Age Press printed underground literature on thin paper and the banned works of Leo Tolstoy. Work continued when he returned home in 1908.

TCHERTKOV, Madame Elizabeth (c1831-1922), mother of Vladimir Tchertkov* and friend of Tsar Alexander II, lived in Russia and from 1870 had a summer home Slavanka (Sunrise site) in Southbourne's Belle Vue Road. Her husband Count Gregory was executed during the 1917 Revolution whilst she escaped penniless to Finland. In 1920 she reached Southbourne where she died in 1922 aged 90.

TENNANT, Stephen (1906-1987), 1st Lord Glenconner's eccentric son who was a Twenties' Bright Young Thing, loved Bournemouth and tried to have his house, Wilsford Manor in Wiltshire where he was born, moved to the town. When told this was impossible he had sand dumped in the garden in front of a painted backdrop and declared that Bournemouth had come to him.

During the Second World War, when his house was occupied by the Red Cross, he took a flat at Sunbury Court in Branksome Wood Road where he could enjoy the view of the Upper Pleasure Gardens. His weekend guests, who often dined with him at the Norfolk Hotel, included Cyril Connolly and Rosamund Lehmann. Shortly afterwards Nancy Mitford depicted him as Cedric Hampton in her novel *Love in a Cold Climate*.

As late as the 1970s he loved shopping in Bournemouth where he often bought scarves and materials in Bright's (now Dingles) and lunched at the Royal Bath Hotel. His long hennaed hair was looked after by a hairdresser summoned from Otis hairdressers below Bewlay tobacconist two doors up from WH Smith in The Square.

THOMAS, Alan G (1911-1992), bookseller and antiquarian book fair founder, lodged in Boscombe at the age of 16 when working at Horace G Commin^ where former customers included Aubrey Beardsley*, DH Lawrence* and Lawrence of Arabia. The shop, selling new and second hand books, was run by Commin from 1891 until his early death in 1911. A later owner Ernest Cooper sold the business in 1936 on generous terms to Thomas.

A customer in the 1930s was Lawrence Durrell* who spent long hours on the beach in deep discussion with Thomas and who often visited his home. Durrell admired Thomas for his "wonderful historic sense" and indeed at Boscombe he was aware of his proximity to the former home of the Shelley* family.

When Larry, as Thomas called him, left for Corfu he started throwing out papers and Thomas managed to save from the wastepaper basket the corrected proofs of *Pied Piper of Lovers*. Later Lawrence wrote from Greece to demand some of his other papers which Thomas reluctantly sent. These were subsequently burnt by Nazi troops which led to Lawrence making Thomas his archivist. The Durrell papers were slowly assembled in the loft of Thomas's new married home at 7a Wimborne Road (since demolished). Lawrence would sometimes visit and spend days in the loft reliving the past. Later a large part of the collection was sent out to Lawrence in Cyprus for him to write *Bitter Lemons* and then returned. Choosing to keep the papers at home rather than the shop paid off as Commin's was damaged during the worst German wartime raid when Beales and the Metropole were hit. In 1969 Thomas edited *Spirit of Place: Letters and Essays on Travel* (Faber 1969) for Durrell who dedicated his second novel *Panic Spring* to him in return for proof reading.

Around 1957 Thomas and his wife Shirley drove to Lawrence's new home in the South of France to collect more papers and in 1981 Thomas co-authored *Lawrence Durrell: an illustrated checklist*. The papers once in the loft are now at the Morris Library of Southern Illinois University. Thomas's own Durrell papers were presented to the British Library.

In 1956 Thomas had sold the shop to John Ruston* and from his home Thomas published a series of antiquarian catalogues with covers designed by Kenneth Hatts* who was also responsible for the distinctive Alan G Thomas letterhead.

But within a decade life became difficult when Thomas's wife Ella went missing. He last saw her when she asked for some money to go shopping. Some of her clothes were found on the Purbeck cliff top but she was never found. In 1965 he moved to Chelsea where he was to live with his second wife Shirley. There in 1975 he wrote *Fine Books: Pleasures and Treasures* and *Great Books and Book Collectors.*

He was a striking figure with a huge beard; in winter he walked about the town in a caped overcoat and a Sherlock Holmes hat. On special occasions he wore a waistcoat which had belonged to William Morris whom he admired and resembled. On his 70th birthday in 1981 Thomas's friends published *Fine books and book collecting* by Christopher de Hamel and Richard A Linenthal in his honour.

THOMPSON, Flora (1876-1947), author of *Lark Rise to Candleford* and its sequels, was just married in 1903 when she moved to 4 Sedgely Road in Winton so that her husband John could take up a position at Bournemouth Post Office where he had worked in 1891. Shortly afterwards the couple moved next door to another new rented house, number six. She enjoyed exploring the countryside including nearby Talbot Village. Although work had begun on Winton Banks there was still Malmesbury Farm opposite alongside St Luke's Church. Their first child Winifred was born in 1903 and baptised at St John's Church in Moordown.

A major event in 1907 was the opening of Winton Library which had a crucial influence on her. "For the first time in my life I had access to a good public library and slipped in, like a duck slipping into water, and read almost everything" she recalled. In 1909, now with a second child Henry, they moved to 2 Edgehill Road which they named Grayshott Cottage after the Hampshire village where Flora had worked at the Post Office. When her husband became union secretary he bought a typewriter which Flora started using. In 1911 she won a writing competition in *Ladies Companion* magazine and the following January published a short story *The Toft Cup*. This gave her confidence although it was 25 years before she started writing her three *Candleford* books.

In 1912 she won another *Ladies Companion* competition which involved writing a criticism of a poem by Ronald Macfie about the Titanic. As a result Dr Macfie visited her at Winton and they became friends. On his death in 1931 Flora wrote: "The bright day is done and we are for dark". In 1915 the family moved to 42 Frederica Road, which they also called Grayshott Cottage, and in August the following year they moved to Liphook in Hampshire.

THORNDIKE, Russell (1885-1972), actor and writer, joined his older sister Sybil Thorndike to stay with his great aunt at Kinson House (flats site in main road west of Kinson Grove). She was a great granddaughter of smuggler Isaac Gulliver* who once lived at Kinson House and this probably inspired Russell to write *Dr Syn*, a Victorian smuggling melodrama which in 1927 he starred in before taking the production around the country and abroad. In 1963 Dame Sybil, who was patron of the Bournemouth Drama Centre, gave a poetry recital at the Palace Court Theatre^.

THORNEYCROFT FOWLER, Ellen (1860-1929), novelist. She moved to Bournemouth with her husband Alfred Felkin in 1916 and lived first at Emo Lodge (site now flats) on north-corner of Clarendon and Portarlington crossroads and then for the rest of their lives at nearby 25 Marlborough Road (site now flats). They called this house Mershire Lodge after the fictional county in Ellen's novels. By then she had a feminist reputation due to her last two books *Miss Fallowfield's Fortune* and *Her Ladyship's Conscience.*

At Westbourne she wrote *Beauty and Bands* (1920), *The Lower Pool* (1923) and her last book *Signs and Wonders* (1926) which was a collection of short stories including one set in the New Forest. Ellen's uncle was godfather to Merton Russell-Côtes* and in 1919 he invited her to the opening of the Russell-Côtes Art Gallery & Museum. She was unable to attend due to poor health which may have curtailed her writing in her last years. She died before her husband and was buried in All Saints Churchyard, Branksome Park. Ellen attended St Ambrose Church in Westbourne whilst Alfred went to St Stephen's Church.

TOLKIEN, JRR (1892-1973), academic and author of *The Hobbit* and *Lord of the Rings,* took holidays from the 1950s to 1972 at the Hotel Miramar on the East Cliff. He had room 37 to himself, as he worked so much, whilst his wife Edith stayed in 39. The climate was good for her arthritis. On Sundays they attended the Sacred Heart Church.

In 1968 they suddenly bought a bungalow Woodridings 19 Lakeside Road (since demolished) just over the border in Poole and took up residence. For the first time they enjoyed central heating and a bathroom each. The garage

Lewis Tregonwell

became an office where Joy Hill from his publisher Allen & Unwin would often help with fan mail. The Tolkien Society had been founded and fans rang day and night forgetting time zones. Following his wife's death in a Bournemouth nursing home in 1971 he returned to Oxford. He came back in August 1973 to stay with friends and died of pneumonia. On 13 October 2005, the 50th anniversary of the publication of *Lord of the Rings*, their daughter Priscilla was at the Sacred Heart for a requiem Mass and afterwards read one of her father's poems.

TOWNSEND, Peter (1914-1995), friend of Princess Margaret*, was a pupil at Wychwood School^ where the headmaster was the husband of Frances Yorke-Batley*. Townsend enjoyed watching cricket at Dean Park and with the school attended St Augustin's Church on Sundays.

TREGONWELL, Lewis (1758-1832), founder of Bournemouth, first visited the Bourne Mouth valley in 1796 when patrolling the coast from Poole to the 'Bourne Chine' and inland to Wimborne in his green uniform as captain of the Dorset Rangers and on alert for a Napoleonic invasion. He returned on Thursday 14 June 1810 with his wife Henrietta to show her the Dorset heath land coastal valley. They called at the Tapps Arms (demolished in 1885 to create Post Office Road southern entrance) and decided to build a house by the stream.

The couple, who lived in Cranborne, were at the time staying at Mudeford and on Wednesday 4 July they brought family friend Harriet Grove (see Percy Bysshe Shelley*) to see the chosen spot. Two months later, on 25 September, they purchased the land bounded by Decoy Pond Lane (Exeter Road) and the footpath (Exeter Lane) in the chine from Sir George Tapps*. But it was not until 24 April 1812 that his wife could write in her diary "...went to Bourne. Slept there for first time." It was at her instigation that the land had been purchased and the house, with gothic windows and first known as The Mansion, now forms part of the Royal Exeter Hotel in Exeter Road. The thatched butler's cottage (downhill to the north) was known as Portman Lodge^ after Henrietta's maiden name. (Her father was Henry Portman, grandfather of the 1st Lord Portman*.) The Tregonwells lived in the main house in the summer but after a few years preferred Portman Lodge. In the 1820s and 1830s The Mansion was let to the Dowager Marchioness of Exeter* after whom Exeter Road is named.

The spring journey from Cranborne was by way of Wimborne with a stop at The Crown in Oakley for lunch whilst the horses were fed and rested. On Sundays the couple drove to St James's Church in Poole. They kept two cows in the chine meadow (now Lower Pleasure Gardens).

Although 1810 is taken as the foundation date for Bournemouth it may be that Cliff Cottage, which stood on the opposite side of Exeter Road, was built before 1810 (see Charles Darwin*). There are earlier buildings at Holdenhurst, Boscombe (see Percy Shelley*) and Southbourne (see Lady Strathmore*). Certainly the Tapps Arms, which Tregonwell bought in 1812 and renamed the Tregonwell Arms, had been in existence since at least 1809. The Southampton-Weymouth coach stopped there along with other carriers. A baker called at the hamlet four times a week. Tregonwell is buried in St Peter's churchyard.

TWELLS, Henry (1823-1900), priest and hymn writer, came to the town in January 1890 from Peterborough due to ill health. He assisted at St Stephen's Church and when the new pulpit was installed in June he was the first person to preach from it.

Soon he became aware of an idea for a new church in the north of the parish and in 1891 he wrote to the Vicar offering to build it "in recognition of the countless mercies I have received from Almighty God during a long Life". In November Mrs Twells laid the foundation stone of St Augustin's Church designed by her husband's friend William Butterfield. It was his last church and built of Purbeck stone unlike his famous churches and buildings such as Keble* College.

Although Twells is best known for the hymn *At even when the sun was set*. He also wrote *Not for our sins alone* and *Glorious is thy name* and several poems about Bournemouth including *The Pier is thronged* and *Don't cut down the pines*. On his deathbed it was arranged for a choirboy to stand downstairs in his home and sing *At even when the sun was set*. Canon Twells is remembered at Peterborough Cathedral by a stained glass window and on the cross in front of St Augustin's Church.

TYRELL, Sir Walter (c1065-c1102), alleged assassin of William II. After maybe accidentally fatally shooting the King William 'Rufus' with an arrow during a hunt on 2 August 1100 in the New Forest, Tyrell is said to have fled to Poole and boarded a ship sailing for Europe. Recent research by the historian Arthur Lloyd (1908-2009) indicates that the murder, or accident, took place at Beaulieu and not Canterton so the escape route is unclear. Tyrell's Oak, where he may have hid, was felled to make way for Hurn airport but it has been long believed that, having had his horse reshod backwards at Avon, he crossed the River Stour at Pigshoot in Throop.

U/V

UNDERWOOD, Florence (c1875-1942), women's suffrage campaigner, Women's Freedom League general secretary and from 1909 to 1933 editor of *The Vote*, was the daughter of George Underwood, gilder and picture framer at 88 Commercial Road, (corner of Terrace and Tregonwell Roads junction) where customers included Robert Louis Stevenson*. The family attended Richmond Hill Congregational Church^ where in 1892 Edward Cleal* persuaded her Liberal supporter father George to help form a Fabian Society branch. Florence remained a Fabian long after the small group folded two years later. Her association with Bournemouth seems to have ended when her father died in 1924.

VERLAINE, Paul (1844-1896), French poet, arrived in Bournemouth from Lincolnshire at the end of May 1876 to teach drawing at St Aloysius School (site of Premier Lodge) in Poole Road. He had no art experience but had to supervise a class drawing squares, cubes and pyramids. One pupil at the time was Raphael Merry Del Val*. Verlaine probably moved with the school in March 1877 to nearby 24 Surrey Road (corner of Queen's Road). The house is called Villa Remington after the headmaster the Revd Frederick Remington, an Anglican convert to Rome, who taught French. The school attended the Sacred Heart Church where Verlaine met Father Anderton, Cardinal Manning's nephew. Verlaine loved walking along the cliffs and during his time at the school he wrote two poems: *Bournemouth* and *La Mer de Bournemouth*. He left for Paris in September 1877.

von HÜGEL, Friedrich (Baron) (1852-1925), Roman Catholic modernist theologian who married the sister of Lord Herbert*. In 1870 von Hügel stayed at Portman Lodge^ and later visited Boscombe in order to study Greek with the scholar Frederick Apthorp Paley*. In 1901 Friedrich came from his Hampstead home to be at the deathbed of his sister Pauline von Hügel*.

Paul Verlaine

Baroness Pauline von Hügel

von HÜGEL, Baroness Pauline (1858-1901), founder of Corpus Christi School in Boscombe. At the age of 20 she came to Bournemouth with her widowed mother Elizabeth and a friend Ellen Redmayne. They lived at Moorfield (since demolished) on the corner of Richmond Hill and Bodorgan Road.

Later Pauline and Miss Redmayne moved to 221 Christchurch Road (Corpus Christi School site) in Boscombe (opposite Gloucester Road) which she called Loreto after the Italian town where the Virgin Mary's house has been reassembled.

As a Roman Catholic, Pauline was pleased to be able to attend Mass at the Convent of the Cross which opened in Parkwood Road in 1887. With her help the sisters had an iron chapel purchased from Lord Petre and erected in the grounds. However the chapel was not large enough and so the Baroness purchased a house called Holywood along with two acres for a new church which she decided to call Corpus Christi. She was assisted by Miss Redmayne who had inherited a large sum of money. The foundation stone of the church was laid in 1895 and the completed building opened on Our Lady's Birthday 8 September 1896.

An early visitor that autumn was Aubrey Beardsley* who had moved to Boscombe in August. He described the building as 'beautiful' and in November he was visited by Father Charles de Lapasture SJ from Bournemouth's Sacred Heart Church who had been given responsibility for the Boscombe church. Beardsley found him "most charming and sympathetic".

In the early days the Baroness played the harmonium and directed the choir. At Easter 1897 the church officially became Boscombe's Roman Catholic parish church.

W

WADE, Eustace (1901-1988), priest and father of Virginia Wade. Shortly after being forced by the German occupation to leave Paris, where he was British Embassy chaplain, he was in 1942 made vicar of Holy Trinity Church^. He knew the church as a child when he stayed with his aunt. He had packed Sunday congregations made up of residents and service people including Americans. He was responsible for maintaining at the once evangelical church what he called "a central position" in worship which endured until the church closed in 1973.

In 1945 his daughter Virginia, the 1977 Wimbledon tennis champion, was born at a Parkstone nursing home and baptised at the Church of the Holy Trinity^. Her first eleven months were spent at Holy Trinity Vicarage where there was a tennis court. In 1947 her father took up an appointment in South Africa where he became Archdeacon of Durban.

WALLACE, Edgar (1875-1932), journalist and prolific author, stayed at the Branksome Towers Hotel (since demolished) at Branksome Chine which led him to use the area for much of his novel *Mr Justice Maxell* (first published in 1923 and republished as *Take-a-Chance Anderson*). In the story Timothy Anderson keeps watch in the garden where there is a disused well. The clock, which he heard strike midnight and one o'clock, belongs to St Ambrose Church in West Cliff Road. The 'Parade Drug Store' is probably Taylor's (103 Poole Road) in Westbourne which had a distinctive private lamp post with a red light outside. A lodging 'Vermont House' was in Western Avenue. The concert featured probably took place at the Winter Gardens^. Later, during his years as an active Liberal, Wallace returned to open a bazaar in Bournemouth.

WARD, Leslie (1888-1978), artist, was in 1895 awarded a scholarship to Drummond Road Art School^ where he studied under Lister Lobley. Later he became a teacher there and in 1913 moved to the new Bournemouth School of Art at the Lansdowne where he stayed until retirement.

From his early twenties he was an exhibitor at the Royal Academy of Arts and a member of the Royal Society of Painter-Etchers. His home was 22 Grant's Avenue near St Mary's Church (now Bourne Spring Centre) where he worshipped. His drawing of the Robert Louis Stevenson* house prior to its destruction in the Second World War is much reproduced. His many pictures of Poole Harbour are a result of having a small boat which he sailed with his friend Eustace Nash*. Both were founder members of the Bournemouth Arts Club. Ward's works includes etching, watercolour and oil.

WEBB, Beatrice (1858-1943), welfare state founder, was sent at the age of 16 to Stirling House boarding school at the top of Bath Hill (petrol station site). Oscar Beringer* was the music teacher.

Beatrice's father had asked two admirals, George Grey*and James Sulivan* to keep an eye on her. The latter took Beatrice to Holy Trinity Church^ on Sundays rather than the high church St Peter's which the school favoured. Although she disagreed with Sir James's religious views she liked the Holy Trinity's Vicar, Philip Eliot*. She was confirmed and made her first communion.

In 1886 she returned with her father to spend three winters at Kildare (since demolished to make way for car park) next to the Royal Bath Hotel. A depressed 28 year old Beatrice looked out of her window on "that hateful grey sea" but then came what she always considered to be a turning point in her life when she received a request from the editor of *The Pall Mall Gazette* asking permission to print her letter on unemployment as an article.

In 1909, as a member of the Royal Commission on the Poor Law, she published her Minority Report which laid the foundation of the modern welfare state. In 1910 she spoke about her ideas at St Peter's Hall (now a night club) at a meeting sponsored by the Poole & Bournemouth branch of the National Committee for the Prevention of Destitution. Tickets could be 'procured only' in the book department of Bright's (now Dingles). She ended her address by appealing to those who were leading comfortable lives in Bournemouth to do all they could to help. During questions Beatrice said she did not look forward to any immediate diminution in costs as schemes cost money but suggested that the question was whether one cared to prevent destitution.

In 1926 Beatrice and her husband Sidney Webb* stayed at the Empress Hotel (now NatWest) at the bottom of Richmond Hill during the TUC gathering at Bournemouth Town Hall.

In September 1934, whilst her husband was abroad she stayed at the Royal Bath Hotel. Writing to Sidney she thought of her old winter home next door and wondered at her present good fortune. Early in the morning she again heard the waves breaking on the sand below and found it a "delicious and satisfying sound" bringing back the memory of February 1886 when the waves

The Osborne in Exeter Road, where Sidney Webb convalesced

Beatrice Webb

seemed to express to her "the despair of suppressed passion and a hopeless outlook". She recalled the letter from the *Pall Mall Gazette* and how that "minute encouragement became the signpost which told me I was on the right road to the end I had in view. After that I never looked back or to the left or to the right".

When the couple stayed at the Highcliff Hotel during the 1937 Labour Party Conference, Beatrice called on old friends Athelston Rendall* and 90 year old Benjamin Jones* who she had known in London when she was living in Bournemouth in the 1880s.

WEBB, Sidney (Lord Passfield) (1859-1947), social reformer and member of the first Labour cabinet. At the end of November 1890 he was taken ill with scarlet fever and his future wife Beatrice (Webb*) encouraged him to convalesce in Bournemouth. He arrived at The Osborne boarding house in Exeter Road (corner of Priory Road and now the BIC^) with Graham Wallas who had also written one of the original Fabian essays.

Sidney spent the daytime out walking and the rest of his time reading by the fire but for him life inside the house was "soul destroying" and he considered that the "moral and intellectual atmosphere" was lowered by the presence of so many idle people. He wrote to Beatrice: "I must get the Liberal Party to add to its programme the Abolition of Scarlet Fever." He was engaged in an effort to turn the Fabian Society into a pressure group within the Liberal Party and added: "I think you are duty bound to join the Fabian Society." His wife became its most famous member.

WELENSKY, Sir Roy (1907-1991), Prime Minister of Federation of Rhodesia and Nyasaland, moved from Zimbabwe to Blandford Forum following independence in 1980. He is buried in the Reform Jewish section of Kinson Cemetery.

WEST, Arthur (1876-1912), Titanic disaster victim, was a floor walker at JJ Allen department store (now the Quadrant Centre) who sold his house in Paisley Road intending to start a fruit cultivation business in Florida. When his wife Ada and children Barbara and Constance were in the lifeboat he let himself down on a rope to give them a flask of hot milk before climbing back to be drowned on the sinking liner. Arthur, whose body was never found, has a memorial in Truro Cathedral. Barbara lived until 2007.

WEST, William (1760-c1820), farmer, moved to Muscliff Farm in 1800 with his family. He won approval from neighbours by relaying the muddy and rutted Muscliff Lane. Being well-read and a recent medal winner for a farming essay competition run by the government, the 'wise farmer' was soon called on to be the local spokesperson as fears rose over the 1802 Christchurch Enclosure Act. West met the Enclosure Commissioners^ when they were sitting at Ringwood to receive representations. As a result areas now known as Meyrick Park, Queens Park, Kings Park, Redhill Common and Seafield Gardens, although assigned to Sir George Tapps*, were designated as turbury commons where the poor could continue to collect wood and cut turves for fires.

Today these tracts of land are held in trust by the Five Parks Charity. The following year William Hunt, who had come to Muscliff with the Wests, was press ganged into the Navy whilst on the beach at Bournemouth helping fishermen land a mackerel catch. When he returned to Muscliff thirteen years later he found that William West had left in 1804 after a loan had suddenly been called in due to a death in the family.

WHISTLER, James Abbott McNeill (1834-1903), painter, spent Christmas 1896 at the Belle Vue Hotel (on part of the Pavilion site opposite the Pier). This was the year he had been widowed and he arrived on Christmas Eve accompanied by publisher Thomas Fisher Unwin, his wife Jane and Elizabeth Robins, wife of art critic Joseph Pennell who arrived the next day. He joined Whister as he wandered around the town on Christmas Day carrying a little paint box looking unsuccessfully for watercolour subjects. At Christmas dinner he found the vegetables watery and the wine poor and started thinking of his room in the Rue du Bac. Conversation revolved around an article the *Saturday Review* by Walter Sickert attacking both Pennell and Whistler. The latter had first seen it whilst on the train to Bournemouth and successful legal action followed in the New Year.

They enjoyed several drives, one to a pub in Poole, but Pennell went alone to see Aubrey Beardsley* at Boscombe. Whistler knew Beardsley was unwell and did not like to see suffering.

WHITLOCK, Percy (1903-1946), composer and organist who studied under Vaughan Williams at London's Royal College of Music. Disappointed at not being promoted at Rochester Cathedral where he was assistant organist at 17, Whitlock moved to Bournemouth in 1930 to be Director of Music at St Stephen's Church. He had just composed his plainsong *Magnificat* and *Nunc Dimittis* and he consolidated his reputation with his compositions at St Stephen's Church although the choir was just sixteen boys and one alto.

Within a year he married soprano Edna Kingdon. From 1932 Whitlock took a second post of Municipal Organist performing at The Pavilion and working with Sir Dan Godfrey* and the Bournemouth Municipal Orchestra. In 1935, when this became a full-time post he resigned from St Stephen's Church. That year he produced the *Song of Bournemouth*. Many of his compositions were for the orchestra. He also wrote a music column for the *Bournemouth Daily Echo* under the name Kenneth Lark and contributed to *The Musical Times*, *The Organ* and *Musical Opinion*. During the Thirties he gave recitals at several leading London churches.

In 1940 he played *La Marseillaise* at the Labour Party Conference when the former French premier Leon Blum addressed delegates who were endorsing the new Churchill war coalition. When rejected for active service due to high blood pressure, Whitlock worked for two years in the Bournemouth food control office in The Pavilion and in 1942 composed *A March for the Phoebe* in honour of the naval vessel adopted by the town. The BBC Home Service broadcast seventeen of his organ recitals from The Pavilion. He also played at a BBC Promenade Concert under his friend Sir Henry Wood.

At the end of his life he was working as secretary to the Municipal Orchestra conductor Monty Birch. Whitlock's home from 1935 was Brinklea Cottage 10 Wimborne Road where he had an organ with the pipes in the cellar and chimneys. He died there on May Day 1946 having undertaken his last public recital on Good Friday at The Pavilion. His *Communion Service in G* remains a standard Mass setting at St Stephen's Church.

WILDE, Oscar (1854-1900), writer and playwright, was so impressed in 1878 by the many art treasures placed around the Royal Bath Hotel by its owner Merton Russell-Côtes* that he wrote in the visitors book: "You have built and fitted up with the greatest beauty and elegance, a palace, and filled it with gems of art, for the use and benefit of the public at hotel prices."

After spending the early part of 1883 in Paris, where he met Verlaine*, Wilde arrived in Bournemouth on Saturday 3 November ready to speak on The House Beautiful that evening at the Theatre Royal^ in Albert Road. However the talk had been booked for earlier in the day leaving a disappointed audience. He returned to speak on the following Friday and Saturday after wondering if he would ever be forgiven in Bournemouth. He stayed at Newlyn's Family Hotel (now the Royal Exeter Hotel). A fortnight later he became engaged to his future wife Constance Lloyd.

In 1888 he lectured on Thomas Chatterton at the Shaftesbury Hall (later West's Pictures cinema; now the Burlington Arcade site).

Oscar Wilde

Chang Woo Gow

WILHELM II (1859-1941), German Kaiser who following a State Visit in 1907 spent three weeks at Highcliffe Castle to the east of Christchurch. Some of his retinue stayed at the Royal Bath Hotel. The Kaiser, who toured the area in a scarlet Daimler, drove through the Lower Pleasure Gardens and along the promenade. Two days later he drove through the town. He twice visited Lord Malmesbury* at Hurn Court where Holdenhurst and Throop villagers gathered at the gates. During his second brief visit he planted a tree. At Kinson the car became stuck in the Kinson Brook ford in Millhams Lane and farm workers Jesse Short and Bill Hicks had to push the Daimler out of the water. Sitting next to the chauffeur on every drive was William McArdle, the Bournemouth Daimler agent. One evening the band of the German Royal Yacht *Hohenzollern* played at the Winter Gardens^.

WILLIAMS, Anthony (1892-1975), Bishop of Bermuda, was appointed Vicar of St Peter's Church in 1946. In the post-war years he faced a lack of clergy and money in the parish but during the 1951 Festival of Britain over 3,000 people visited the church to see a play by Christopher Fry*. In 1956 Williams was made Bishop of Bermuda. He was consecrated in Westminster Abbey in September but stayed on at St Peter's Church as its mitred vicar until November.

WILSON, Harold (1916-1995), Prime Minister. In 1974, having just become premier for the second time, he addressed the Post Office Workers' conference at the Winter Gardens^ where he received a standing ovation. He also lunched at the Highcliff Hotel and was guest at tea, hastily arranged by Cllr Ron Whittaker, with Labour Party members at Labour Hall^ (since demolished for flats) before flying back to London from Hurn Airport.

In 1981, when he was Lord Wilson and had just published his book *The Chariot of Israel*, he addressed a meeting in the Menorah Suite in Glen Fern Road. Afterwards he stayed a night at the Royal Bath Hotel.

WILSON, Sir Horace (1882-1972), co-architect of appeasement who accompanied Neville Chamberlain to his two meetings with Hitler as well as making a solo visit. The son of a furniture dealer, Wilson attended Kurnella (now Lingwood) boys' school at 30 Tregonwell Road. When a top civil servant he continued to live with his wife and children at 8 Byron Road in Boscombe. As war approached the *Bournemouth Daily Echo* described him as "carrying the world's peace hopes". His death at home was followed, at his request, by a private funeral at Bournemouth Crematorium.

WIMBORNE, Lady Cornelia (1847-1927), Lord Randolph Churchill's sister who in 1868 married Sir Ivor Guest (1st Baron Wimborne). His seat was Canford and the couple's seaside house was Branksome Dene (now Zetland Court) in Alumhurst Road built in 1860 and designed by Edward Buckton Lamb, architect of the new Royal National Hospital in St Stephen's Road. Among guests at both houses was Cornelia's nephew Winston Churchill*.

WINDSOR, Duke of. See Edward VIII*.

WINN, Anona (1904-1994), early radio personality who chaired *The Petticoat Line* and regularly appeared on *Twenty Questions*. Her home from 1980 was the Queen's Park Nursing Home at 7 Queen's Park Gardens. Having started as an opera singer she enjoyed sitting in a chair singing old popular songs.

WINNINGTON-INGRAM, Arthur (1858-1946), Bishop of London, preached at St Peter's, St Augustin's and St Swithun's Churches to raise funds for the East London Church Fund. His mother lived in Cavendish Place. In 1923, he dedicated the east window of Holy Trinity Church^. In 1939, after 39 years as Bishop of London, he spent each winter at the Crag Head Hotel (rebuilt as flats) where he found butter rationing difficult. He often celebrated or preached at St Peter's Church where the vicar Hedley Burrows* was an old friend. The bishop enjoyed golf at Queen's Park. Once, having sent a lump of earth into the air, he turned to local caddie Len Loader and said: "My boy did you see that sod fly?" Young Len replied: "I regret having to correct you My Lord but I must point out that you never touched the ruddy ball."

WOLLSTONECRAFT, Mary (1759-1797), first feminist author and mother of Mary Shelley*, whose remains were brought from a London churchyard in St Pancras to St Peter's churchyard and placed in the Shelley family tomb in 1851.

WOO GOW, Chang (1846-1893), Chinese giant. Eight foot tall and speaking four languages, he toured the world before living briefly in Derby Road and settling at Moyuen (now Ashleigh Hotel) in Southcote Road in 1890 to run a Chinese tearoom and bazaar. The house had an extra tall door and windows. He quickly became very well-known in the town. On Sundays he attended East Cliff Congregational Church. After suffering from suspected tuberculosis, and just four months after his Australian wife's death, he died in the arms of photographer Robert Day* junior. The coffin, measuring eight foot and four inches long and two foot and six inches wide, required eight bearers.

WOOD, Arthur (1875-1953), composer of *The Archers* signature tune *Barwick Green*, was a flautist with the Bournemouth Municipal Orchestra under the baton of Sir Dan Godfrey*. In 1902, a year before moving to London, he published his first orchestral work *Three Old Dances*.

WOOLDRIDGE, Ian (1932-2007), award-winning sports journalist, represented New Milton Boys' Club in the Bournemouth Table Tennis League. In 1953 he left the *New Milton Advertiser* for the *Bournemouth Times* where after a year he became sports editor of both the *Bournemouth Times* and its sister paper the *Poole & Dorset Herald*. He moved to Fleet Street in 1956 for a job on the *News Chronicle*. When the paper sent him back to Bournemouth to cover a football match at Dean Court he met the *Daily Herald* correspondent John Bromley who became a life long friend. In 1961 Ian joined the *Daily Mail* where he was to write for the rest of his life and work closely with David English*. Wooldridge received the London Press Club's Edgar Wallace* Award a year before his death.

WREN, Percival Christopher (1875-1941), novelist, who in 1927, a year after *Beau Geste* was turned into a film, bought Westwood 9 Elgin Road which had been built three years earlier and had a garden adjoining Meyrick Park. He added the extension, allegedly to represent a Foreign Legion fort, before moving in 1934. It was later home of Bennett Beale, son of John Elmes Beale*.

Y

YATES, Edmund (1831-1894), journalist and novelist, sometimes stayed at the Royal Bath Hotel and after his last visit in 1892, when in poor health, he wrote in the visitors' book: "A charming hotel, excellently conducted, perfect in comfort, cleanliness and cookery." The delighted owner Merton Russell-Côtes* used the quote in an advertisement after the writer's death two years later.

YORKE-BATLEY, Frances (c1906-1996), renowned theatrical hostess, was wife of the Revd William Yorke-Batley who between 1924 and 1938 was Headmaster of Wychwood School^. After a decade as rector of Corfe Castle, the couple returned to Bournemouth and in 1949 he was invited by the Actors' Church Union to become Chaplain at The Pavilion.

A custom developed for actors to be invited to Sunday tea at the Yorke-Batley house at 15 Keswick Road in Boscombe where they played croquet and sat for a group photograph. In 1960 her husband died and Leslie Crowther, who had been an early visitor when on tour, persuaded Mrs Yorke-Batley to continue the custom. The last tea was in October 1989. In 1990 Patrick Fyffe (who played Dame Hilda Bracket), Barry Howard (Barry Stuart-Hargreaves in *Hi-de-Hi!*) and Leslie Crowther were present when the Lord Lieutenant of Dorset presented Mrs Yorke-Batley with the British Empire Medal for services to the theatrical profession.

BIBLIOGRAPHY

Barker, John *The Founders of Bournemouth* (Bournemouth Local Studies 1999)
Battiscombe, Georgina *John Keble: a study in limitations* (1963)
Brawn, Dale *The Court of Queen's Bench of Manitoba, 1870-1950: A Biographical History* (University of Toronto Press 2006)
Bray, Winifred M *Westbourne: A Personal View* (Bournemouth Local Studies Publications 1983)
Brittain, Vera *England's Hour* (Macmillan/Futura 1981)
Buckle, George *The Life of Benjamin Disraeli: Earl of Beaconsfield* (John Murray 1920)
Buehrle, Marie C *Rafael, Cardinal Merry del Val* (The Bruce Publishing Company 1957)
Carpenter, SC *Winnington-Ingram* (Hodder 1949)
Cline, Sally *Radclyffe Hall: A Woman called John* (John Murray 1997)
Dale, 'Farmer' *Reminiscences of Stourfield* (Dorset County Council 1975)
Davies, Peter *Art in Poole & Dorset* (Poole Historical Trust 1987)
Driberg, Tom *Ruling Passions* (Cape 1977)
Drummond Wolff, Henry *Rambling Recollections* (Macmillan 1908)
Edwards, Elizabeth *Bournemouth Past* (Phillimore 1998)
Edwards, Elizabeth *Famous Folk of Bournemouth, Poole and the Surrounding Area* (Natula 2006)
Essex, Rosamund *Woman in a Man's World* (Sheldon 1977)
Fisher, John *Tony Hancock: The Definitive Biography* (HarperCollins 2008)
Fox, Ernest *Contracts and Contacts* (Estates Gazette 1943)
Hatts, Leigh *Exploring the Bournemouth Coast Path* (Countryside 2005)
Hatts, Leigh *The Fabians in Bournemouth* (Bournemouth Fabian Society 1999)
Hawkins, Desmond *Shelley's First Love* (Kyle Cathie 1992)
Hawkins, Desmond *The Grove Diaries* (University of Delaware 1995)
Johnson, Stanley *Stanley I Presume?* (Fourth Estate 2009)
Leake, David *Springbourne* (Bournemouth Local Studies Publications 1990)
Legg, Rodney *Bournemouth: The Good Old Days* (Halsgrove 2003)
MacDonald, Frederick W *The Life of William Morley Punshon* (Hodder 1888)
Mate, Charles & Riddle, Charles *Bournemouth 1810-1910* (Mate 1910)
McInnes, Peter *Freddie My Friend* (Caestur Books 1995)
McQueen, Ian *Bournemouth St Peter's* (Dorset Publishing Company 1971)
Moore, Wendy *Wedlock: How Georgian's Britain worst husband met his match* (Weidenfeld 2009)

Mulchrone, Vincent *Care & Charisma: The Carlton Tradition* (The Carlton 1975)
Norman, Andrew *Dunshay, Reflections on a Dorset Manor House* (Halsgrove 2005)
Perry, Anthony *Ellen's Bournemouth Years - The story of a forgotten writer Ellen Thornycroft Fowler* (Brewin Books 2000)
Peters, John *Bournemouth Then & Now* (Blandford Press 1978)
Popham, David & Rita *The Book of Bournemouth* (Barracuda 1985)
Pugh, Peter *The Royal Bath: A History* (Cambridge Business Publishing 1988)
Samuel, Olive J *Boscombe Manor* (Natula 2004)
Southam, Diana *The Trials of Radclyffe Hall* (Weidenfeld & Nicolson 1998)
Sturgis, Matthew *Aubrey Beardsley: A Biography* (Harper Collins 1998)
Sumner, Heywood *Cuckoo Hill: the Book of Gorley* (Bellow 1987)
Townsend, Peter *Time and Chance; An Autobiography* (Collins 1998)
Whittaker, Ron & Challen, Peter *Lives and Times of the Mayors of Bournemouth 1890-2000* (Bournemouth Borough Council 2000)
Williams, Anthony *From A to B (Antrim to Bermuda)* (Dorset Publishing Company 1972)
Young, JA *Victorian Boscombe* (Bournemouth Local Studies Publications 1983)
Young, JA *The Story of Southbourne* (Bournemouth Local Studies Publications 1989)
Young, David S *The Story of Bournemouth* (Robert Hale 1957)

INDEX of people without individual entries

Abdy Lady 132
Adams, George 48
Albany, Duchess of 29,133
Allison, William 86
Anne, Princess 41,53,69
Armstrong, Louis 16
Arnold, Thomas 16
Ashley, Rosalie 127
Attallah, Niam 112
Avebury, Lord 47

Baden-Powell, Sir Robert 19,130
Bartlett, Bill 132
Beale, Bennett 173
Bearne, Father David 23
Beaton, James 69
Beecham, Sir Thomas 123
Beerbohm Tree, Sir Herbert 141
Bellamy, David 52
Belsky, Franta 25
Bennett, Revd William 25
Bernadotte, Count Folke 29
Bickel, Leslie 100
Blum, Leon 169
Blyton, Enid 115
Boal, William 40
Bodley, Sir Thomas 30
Bonfield, Terry 130
Boswell, James 64
Bott, Thomas 31
Bowness, Sir Alan 99
Brassey, TH 20
Bright, Percy 32,87
Brooke, Sir Alan (Field Marshal Viscount Alanbrooke) 40
Brooke, Richard 33
Burras, Edith 92
Butler, Reg 99
Butterfield, William 160
Caine, Michael 15
Campbell, Annie 116
Carlyle, Thomas 49
Caroline, Princess 102
Castleman, William 48
Chamberlain, Neville 17,40,107,171
Churchill, Randolph 55,172
Clarendon, Lord 107
Clark, Sir Kenneth 133
Coburn, Charles 77
Cockerell, FP 127
Cody, Sam 132
Connolly, Cyril 155
Cooper Dean, Joseph 66,68
Corbett, Harry 43
Corbett, Matthew 43
Cordle, John 80,144
Cordrey, Roger 40
Cripps, Sir Stafford 118
Cromwell, Oliver 39
Crowther, Leslie 174
Crumpler, Harry 34
Crundall, Robert 147
Curran, Amelia 140

Day, Emily 47
Day, Mary 47
Day, William 47,48
de Lapasture, Fr Charles 22,163
de Torre Diaz, Count 106
de Vere, Aubrey 154
Defoe, Daniel 43
Depp, Johnny 15

Devonshire, Georgina, Duchess of 66
Dodman, Frank 99
Douglas, Lord Alfred 44
Druitt, Herbert 50
Druitt, John 50
Druitt, Montague 50
Druitt, W Harvey 50
Dunn, Sir Vivian 110

Edwards, Robert (Bob) 143
Elizabeth II 30,104,112
Exeter, 1st Marquess 61

Fairweather, George 78
Ferrier, Kathleen 52,100
Fisher, Dr James 61
Foot, Michael 92
Forte, Lord 65
Franz Josef I 57
Freeman, Robert 24
Fry, Elizabeth 66
Furlong, Monica 61
Fyffe, Patrick 174

Gardner, Margery 82
Garnett, Richard 138
Gilbert Scott, Sir George 30,136
Goodwin, Joe 80
Granville, Lord 66,67
Gray, John 22,23
Griffiths, Jim 80
Grove, Harriet 140,159

Hammond, Henry A 46
Hankinson, Cyril 79
Harcourt, Sir William 52
Harewood, 2nd Earl 120
Harsant, Dr JD 23,24
Hawker, WJ 23
Heathcote, Robert 114
Helena Victoria, Princess 104,105
Herbert, Auberon 154
Hicks, David 110
Hicks, Pamela 110
Hockney, David 99
Holland, Clive 78,79
Holmes, Stan 146
Hooper, Edward 102
Hope, Bob 87
Howard, Barry 174
Howard, Lord 114
Hunt, William 168

Jack the Ripper 15,50
Johnson, Boris 91
Johnson, Stanley 91
Johnson, Samuel 64
Jones, Karen 81

Keats, John 40
Kemp-Welch, Edith 92
Kent, Duke of 119
Kerley, Samuel 120
Kilmuir, Lord 55
King, William 50

Lamb, Edward Buckton 172
Landseer, Edward 102
Lang, Rt Revd Cosmo Gordon 95
Lascelles, Lady Emma 120
Lehmann, Rosamund 155
Liszt, Franz 66,127
Lloyd, Arthur 160
Loader, Len 172
Lobley, Lister 164
Londesborough, Lord 107

Mabley, Brian 52
McArdle, William 171
Macfie, Ronald 157